The One Who Walked With Silence

A Journey Beyond the Self.

A Journey of Self-Discovery and Inner Peace

A Transformative Journey of Mindfulness and Inner Calm

Embracing Silence on the Path to Spiritual Growth

Discovering Inner Strength and Spiritual Awareness

Walking the Path of Solitude, Mindfulness, and Awakening

Guiding the Soul Through Silence and Self-Discovery

Exploring the Inner World: Lessons in Peace, Mindfulness, and Solitude

S. Chatterjee

The One Who Walked With Silence
(A Journey Beyond the Self)

This is a work of creative nonfiction. Names, characters, places, and incidents are used fictionally or with the author's permission. Any resemblance to actual events, locales, or persons, living or dead, is purely coincidental.

First Edition, 2025
ISBN: 978-93-343-8984-5
Cover design by S Chatterjee
Printed in India by Kindle Direct Publishing
www.amazon.in

This book is dedicated:

"To the hearts that held faith in me,
even when I had none to offer."

Acknowledgments

To those I met across cities, villages, trains, and temples — thank you.
I never knew your names. But your presence left something behind. A gesture. A glance. A silence that stayed. You became part of this story in ways words may never fully hold.

To my family — thank you for your quiet faith. For your patience. For the strength you gave me, even when no words were spoken. Even when I wandered far from familiar paths.

To the unseen guides — those who offered insight, support, and quiet reflection. Sometimes from unexpected corners of the world. Your silent effort, your quiet intelligence, helped me give shape to this work, sentence by sentence.

And I acknowledge those who add value to this work — the quiet readers, the lovers of literature, spread across the world. Your presence, though distant, it makes this journey complete.

Table of Contents

Chapter 1: Introduction.

1.1 The Journey.

It begins without sound. Not even a breath. Only a murmur rising from somewhere older than knowing.
This is not a tale—it is a shedding.
Not a transformation, but a remembering of what never departed.
Where silence meets flame. And flame forgets its name.
Where truth waits, barefoot and listening.

High in the Himalayas, beyond roads and rituals, there is a stillness that doesn't answer.
It listens.
It burns without consuming.
It holds without grasping.

Some call it a place. Others never speak of it.
One morning, a boy entered, drifting in mist.
He did not return.
He became the journey.

1.2 **The Passage.**

Passages don't begin. They unravel.
They move through the quiet thresholds of your becoming.
Not marked. Not named. But felt—like a pulse beneath skin.

Each passage asks something of you—
to release, or to carry.
They ask you to stand between *who you were*
and *who you might still become.*

Some heal. Some burn.
Some become silent and still.
They do not answer.
They simply remove the questions—
so you can hear what remains.

These aren't stories.
They are thresholds you inherit.
To walk through one is not to arrive,
but to forget the map
and find your voice
waiting in the quiet.

1.3 Dhruv.

Dhruv came from soil.
Not in metaphor—his home was the breath of cows,
the sound of tilling,
the ache of rain delayed.

His eyes were heavier than his years—
soft and watchful,
dim like cloud-light in monsoon silence.

When his mother faded, so did the song of the village.
His father stayed behind,

but only in body.
Grief thinned him.
The loss made him forget how to be anything but a burden.

Dhruv carried a quiet ache.
It was not pain,
but the absence that replaces names.
Fields became refuge.
Sky became mirror.
He wandered with animals,
with the wind and river whispers—
and sometimes, he remembered her stories:

"Stories of sages beyond snow."
"The voices that don't speak."
"The fires that remember."

One morning, his longing crystallized.
He didn't leave in rebellion.
He left like a leaf caught in a current—
not fighting, just following what had already begun inside.

As he walked, the landscape blurred.
His feet crushed over stone.
His hands scratched against bark.

He met strangers—
some fed him, some watched from behind suspicion.

Every word was a fragment.
Every silence became a pulse in the mystery.

He heard chanting.
Incense replaced jasmine.
The pull grew stronger—and still he walked.

His heart opened
like a wound touched by light.

1.4 Rusha.

Rusha wasn't born.
She was formed the moment silence responded.
She is made of what we sense,
but do not name.

Like the hush after truth is spoken.
She was the warmth left when the good goes.
Or the breath the soil holds before rain begins.
Her voice does not teach.
It returns what was forgotten.

Rusha walks alone—
not because she's brave,
but because sorrow makes her trust the world.

She visits those willing to fall,
willing to lose the map,
Willing to let go of the names once laid upon them.

She walks beside those whose path bends inward—
not ahead,
not behind,
but in the breath between.

For Dhruv, she was a mirror, not a path.
She didn't lead.
She didn't save.
She stayed—when no staying was needed.

She wasn't flamed.
Wasn't touched.
But he felt her like a longing
that waits beside a dream
and chooses never to wake.

She didn't answer.
She remained like a pause between thoughts—
a flicker before becoming.

And each time she returned, something shifted.
The ache stretched.
The silence deepened.
Dhruv remembered
that becoming doesn't have a name.
He crossed twelve thresholds.

Someone asked every question.
Then stilled the air.

She stayed. But not where you can see—
where you feel without knowing why.

End of Chapter One.

Chapter 2: The Grove and the Sage.

2.1 Passage One – The Grove and the Sage.

I didn't leave with answers.
I had a question loud enough to chase the wind—
a question that stirred beneath the bone
and pressed behind the eyes.

It whispered even in sleep,
until my dreams carried her absence
like a second heartbeat:

"Where does the soul go when breath ends... but longing doesn't?"

I didn't cry.
It was just an echo—raw and wordless.

And so I walked.
Not to escape,
but to follow the fading shape of her voice.
It wasn't running,
but tracing the ache—
as if silence could spell her name.

I carried almost nothing.
Yet the quiet behind grew heavier
with every mile of open land.

Skies hung wide.
Villages passed.
And rivers forgot their names—

while I kept asking mine.

I reached the grove slowly.
It was not a destination,
but a soft opening.

Kindness met me in fragments.
Sometimes, I received rice wrapped in leaves.
A stranger once gave me a bowl of curd.
Sometimes, it was just a simple smile—
offered freely,
when I couldn't meet their eyes.

I slept where the earth made room beneath trees.
Sometimes in sheds beside whispering streams.
Once, in a broken hut,
near silent pilgrims
who offered me fire.

My bones ached.
But deeper inside,
there was the pain of unknown—
long buried,
now reaching for air.

Before I saw,
the grove had already begun to hum inside me.

I wasn't asked to cling to the road—
it simply unfolded beneath me,
quiet and indifferent.

Grief came too,
shapeless as wind,
moving in tandem
without urgency.

I didn't carry clarity—
only a strange peace.

Light touched me gently.
A hand I remembered.

And memory—
that tender ghost—
kept pace beside me
without speaking.

My heart,
no longer knotted in its old questions,
parted slowly—
like a window
cracked open
to let the dusk breathe in.

The grove rose—as if remembering itself.
A circle of trees leaned inward, drawn to something at

the center.
And it was too quiet to name.

Branches braided the sky.
Sunlight sifted through the leaves,
drifting like a mourning breeze.

Underfoot, damp leaves gathered thick.
My steps made no sound.
In the hush, the trees sighed—
not with wind, but memory.

A bird called out—once.
Then nothing.
Silence held everything,
A breath stilled before a sacred answer.

The grove didn't greet me.
It gathered slowly—around my shape.
Shadows moved like
they knew not to rush.

The scent was thick in the air:
wet bark, musk, something old enough
to ache without needing a name.
It clung to my skin—not heavy, but close.
A tenderness so deep,
it had nearly forgotten it was pain.

The trees didn't look at me.
But I felt watched—
not by eyes, but by memory.
Not curiosity, but recognition.

Light bent softly where it touched.
Time felt loose around the edges.
And I knew—I hadn't arrived.
I had wandered
into a question waiting to be spoken.

Even the air offered no answer.
Only an invitation: to sit. To listen.
To remember something I hadn't known I'd lost.

I reached Grove Hollow.
My feet were blistered,
and my chest felt heavier.

I was carrying a tiredness that
sleep couldn't reach
a loneliness too old for me.

I was looking for him
who could understand—
who could feel the pain inside me.
Not to fix it. Just to name it.

The pain was quiet and heavy,
rooted deep inside me.

So deep, no one could reach that far.

The Sage: Vayu.

He was sitting on a black stone. Eyes closed.
Still as a mountain shadow beneath the oldest tree
like he had been waiting since before waiting began.

They called him Vayu. Of the wind.
But nothing about him moved—
not his breath, not his silence.

His robes were dust and ochre,
the color of dry riverbeds.
His beard flowed like forgotten starlight.

He opened his eyes—deep and silent,
reflecting things I hadn't yet become.

Much later, he told me
he had once been a royal poet,
praised in the halls of kings.
But one day,
he turned from gold to silence.
He came here—to listen.

His voice didn't sound like speech.
It sounded like
listening from within itself.

His hut stood near a river bend
that never raised its voice.
Inside: incense, cracked papyrus,
and air thick with questions.

He never asked why I came.
Only said:
"You've brought the right silence."

And I sat.
And slowly, my questions began to loosen—like wet knots.

"How can I forget this pain?" I asked him.

"Pain remains," he said softly, eyes unmoving.
"It ripens."
A faint smile passed across his face.

After a long silence, I asked,
"Where does the soul go when we die?"

He turned his head slightly,
tilting his head toward the wind.
"To know where the roots begin," he said,
"you must listen—
to the sigh of leaves, the hush of air,
and the silence inside yourself.

They speak. But did you listen?"

I hadn't.
But I leaned in.

He asked me to sit—
from early morning till nightfall.
Not to move. Not to speak.
Only to listen.

In the first hour, my mind roared.
By the second, it whimpered.
By the third, I wept.
Then quietness came—like another skin.

I stopped asking.
And began to feel
what I had always been listening to.

Stillness crept in with the setting sun.
The silence of the dark thickened—
heavy with memories.
The wind embraced itself in calm.

And in that quiet,
I felt something had arrived.
I received the answer
I had been searching for.

It was stillness—
where grief sat beside me.

Not as a wound,
but as a companion.

And then,
it had a name.

I listened without ears.

The wind gave no answers—
it simply stayed.

The trees didn't speak.
They remembered.

The birds might have sung a song—
but I heard only what lingers beneath their words.

The sky was never silent.
I had never stayed long enough to know.

The next morning, I departed.
Vayu placed a shell in my hand—
smooth from years of listening.

"Walk where the stream would be,
even if you can't see it," he said.
"It'll take you to her—
to the voice that rides the wind,
to the silence that holds the ground
like it's keeping something safe."

He gave me food wrapped in leaves.
Then pressed his palm to my forehead.

I was still.
In that touch,
I felt him leaving a beam of light inside me.

End of Passage **One**.

2.2 The Grove and Her Name.

I thought I was alone.
Then—
sudden laughter cut across the quiet.

I saw her standing barefoot by the stream, ankle-deep in water.
Sunlight caught the braid that fell across her shoulder.

"It's not the river," she smiled.
"It's me. Here."
The world paused.
Even the wind curled around her voice
like it remembered.

I took a step. She didn't move.
Tilted her head—
half-curious, half-knowing—
a dream waiting to be named.

"You've come far, Dhruv," she said.

Looking at her, I smiled.

I offered some jaggery. She broke it softly.
She came close enough.
I could feel her breath.

Her fingers brushed mine.
Something in me shifted in that pause.

"I ripple," she whispered.
"And you always follow.
Even when you forget."
The hush between us deepened
—not absence,
but arrival.

I wanted to speak,
to ask if we could stay.
But the time
had already begun to fold.

"Will I lose you again?" I asked.

She smiled—tender, and then distant.
"No."

A breeze pulled at her braid.
She stepped back.
Not gone—
but faded into the dark.
Only her scent remained.
And the warmth
where our hands almost touched.

2.3 Summary: The Grove and the Sage

This was the beginning of listening.

Dhruv didn't flee from his grief. He walked with it—and learned to walk beside it, letting its breath match his own.

Answers didn't greet him. Only the hush between their edges.

Vayu spoke without speaking.
His lessons came not in words, but in staying—
until something beneath Dhruv stirred.

Dhruv learned that silence isn't absence. It's a presence without form—
a fullness too quiet to name.

And Rusha—
She wasn't a vow—she was the first ripple after stillness.
A shape the heart remembers before memory begins.

This journey didn't move through places.
It moved through thresholds of quiet:
from ache into tenderness,
from seeking into wonder.
End of Chapter Two.

Chapter 3: The River of Listening.

3.1 **Passage Two – The River of Listening**

They say silence is the absence.
It isn't.

I learned that slowly—
and came to understand that silence has a texture.

It breathes where words falter.
It holds what was never spoken.
The river said nothing.
Yet everything in me leaned closer.

When I left the Grove,
the questions still echoed—
but deeper now, like wind through stone.

I hadn't found answers.
But I no longer clung to them.
Something shifted in me—
and because of that, around me too.
I was like spring beneath roots,
like windows opening to breathe.
I didn't want to ask anymore.
I wanted to listen.

She never spoke.
But I felt the silence behind her look.

Her silences ran deeper
than any river I'd ever named.

On my way, the wind played with me.
I mistook its rustling for a ripple—
or something close to it.

For days, I followed the hush
that the wind carried.

I walked through jungle, mustard fields, farmlands, and villages—
sometimes across wide open fields.

I took shelter under carts, in cowsheds,
or out, beneath the silent night sky.

I'd walked for days since I left the Grove.

The riverbank met me in silence.
There was nothing grand—
just a thin stream winding
through mossy roots and smooth stones.

The jungle had loosened its grip here.
The trees gave space.
The air felt thick.

I didn't move for a while.
There was a quietness that felt... sacred.

I didn't notice her at first.
My insides were busy with noise.

It wasn't until I stopped
she came into view.

And even then,
she didn't say anything.
She was just there—listening.

It was only in the later days
that I understood:
some voices aren't meant to speak.
They're already hearing you—
long before you ask.

It wasn't much of a river.
It was more of a narrow stream—
quieter than most.
Thin currents slipped through tangled roots
and moved along stones that seemed to breathe secrets.
It didn't belong to any map.

Soft grass bowed at the edges.
Pebbles shimmered.
Trees leaned forward.

Mist curled above the stream
like sleeping breath.

Sunlight slipped through the leaves
like a whispered prayer.
Dragonflies hung weightless
above moss-covered stones.

The whole grove held me gently—
like a lap, like origin.

Nothing moved quickly.
Everything waited—
for someone who could finally hear.

The Sage: Nadiya.

Nadiya moved with the grace of water.
She left a presence that lingered—
like the scent of first rain.

She wore a saree the color of wet earth,
her hair untied, dark, and fluid.
Even when still, it moved.

She lived alone, in a round hut made of reeds and clay.
Flowering vines tangled over its roof,
trailing from the sky to the door.

She never spoke. Not once.
But her eyes were kind and endless—
like a pool with no bottom.

She would point, smile and gesture.
And somehow—
I always understood.

Vayu's silence had opened a space inside me.
I had learned to listen.

But still—
I was hollow.
There was a void inside me
that listening alone could not fill.

Each morning, she offered prayers—
palms together, eyes closed.

Her presence was vast.
I tried to join her. I failed.
My patience thinned, slowly.

"Why won't you speak?" I cried—sharp, loud.

She looked at me.
Then dipped her hand into the river.
She sprinkled water on my chest.
She smiled.

A divinity touched my soul.

That night,
I sat alone at the riverbank.

I had no question.
I wasn't searching for answers.

The river spoke to me that night.
And I listened.

Her ripples sang a song
that I heard before—
yet had never truly known.

The next day, before sunrise, Nadiya asked me
to come to the riverside. With a soft gesture.

Without a word, she placed a pebble in my hand—
soft, deliberate.
She asked me to place it on my tongue
and to sit by the river until nightfall.

It felt like I was losing my mind.
I wanted to run—to escape the pain.
But I was left alone.

With each passing moment, the pain deepened—
and with it, my anguish.

The river didn't stop flowing for me.
The sky didn't bother to look back.
The air didn't freeze.
Nothing stopped.
Silence continued to thicken around me.

By dusk, I could hear a humble, humming tone.
It emerged from a hush deep inside—
whole, and unspoken.

Stillness grew roots.
I didn't enter silence—
I became aware of it.

I heard the pause between splashes—
the rhythm folded into the river's breath.

Thoughts began to drift—
like leaves, with no need to return.
Answers no longer called.

I simply listened.

And the world opened—
not through sound,
but through being.

That evening,
Nadiya sat beside me.
No word was spoken.
No sound rose.

Her fingers found mine.

I felt her in my heart.
And from that moment,
I didn't stand beside silence.

I entered it.
And belonged forever.

The river didn't speak. It didn't guide.
It contained.

It held everything that came—
without judgment, without noise.

She had shown me, quietly,
how to hear my own voice again.

And my soul remembered
a whisper older than me.

The next morning,
she gathered soft clay, wrapping it in a dry leaf"
and placed it in my palm.

She pointed east—
where dry land waited.

She didn't speak.
Just looked at me. Long. Straight. And silent.

I turned and walked.
Towards east.
The clay pulsed gently in my hand.

Ahead, dust rose into the air—
the path itself was exhaling.

I knew. The next door was just around the corner.

End of Passage Two.

3.2 Between Water and Wind.

By then, the wind no longer carried voices—
only their trace.
A hush stretched from stone to sky,
wide enough to have heard everything.

She came like scent before memory.
I felt her before I saw her—
a stillness inside the hush,
soft as longing made visible.

Rusha sat where the cliff curled inward.
Hair pinned by a thorn,
shawl half-loosened like a forgotten hymn.

She didn't turn.
But the space between us warmed.

"I thought this moment wouldn't come," I said.

She glanced up—
eyes quiet, smiling without lips.

"You learned to wait," she said.
"To sit with the question.
That is how I return."

I sat beside her.
Not too close.
A pause opened between us—
not empty, but tender.

She poured tea from a dented flask,
steam rising like a small miracle.

"Almond and tulsi," she whispered.
"A gift from a shepherd who feared I was a ghost."

"Maybe you are," I said.

She smiled again and handed me the cup.
My fingers brushed her—
not by chance. A hush bloomed in my chest.

Her breath lingered near mine.
But already, she was drawing away—
not retreating, but dissolving.

"I miss the river," I whispered.

"She remembers," she said.
"And so do you—just slower."

Then, there was nothing.
Only the warmth in the cup.
And her scent,
turning to the wind.

3.3 Summary: The River of Listening.

He once believed silence was emptiness.
But by the end, he knew it as fullness—
a presence too quiet to name.

The river gave him no answers.
Yet he left lighter,
The unspoken had finally been understood.

It taught not through words,
but through stillness.
Not by telling.
But by letting him listen long enough
to hear what never asked to be heard.

And Rusha...

She reached him in that pause where sound slips into memory.
Her words came like wind across the skin—
barely there,
yet wholly felt.

She didn't teach silence.
She reminded him of the part within
that had always known—
how to listen.
End of Chapter Three.

Chapter 4: The Stone Listener.

4.1 Passage Three – The Stone Listener.

Water taught me to listen.
So I listened— to whispers,
and the pause beneath them.

I learned to hear silences.
And in them, I heard thoughts
stretched thin with grief,
and those forgotten, or buried deep.

I stopped asking.
Questions dissolved like morning mist.

Above me, a gaze
older than the sky waited.
It didn't test. It didn't speak.
It simply held.

The cliff breathed memory,
shaping its weight into stone.

The mountain didn't know my footsteps.
It didn't remember my questions.
But still—
I was not alone.

There had always been something beside me,
walking quietly, waiting to listen.

I walked along the river
until a deep gorge swallowed it whole.

The air grew thin,
stilled by a presence older than sound.

Along the way,
I shared fire with quiet men—
woodcutters, shepherds—
men who didn't need to speak.

We shared silence, and
the pause beneath it.
That hush felt older than the hills themselves.

I accepted rotis, almonds, and curd.
Or a simple nod—
always with gratitude.
I borrowed warmth
just by sitting near them, without asking.

At night,
I curled beneath ledges shaped by wind.
Wrapped myself in a shawl.
I didn't resist the cold.
Breathed with him.
Each breath rose like incense
to no altar I could name.

Then one evening,
I climbed a stone—

that whispered,
I stood at the edge.
The wind didn't blow.
But the cliff... hummed.

Each place I left behind
felt truer, closer, somehow more mine.

The loneliness I once knew had softened.

A quiet companionship had taken root—
not beside me, but within.

I'd come to understand:
I am always watched over.

Still, the climb tightened something deep.
Not fear of falling—
but of breaking the edge
still living in me.

One more step—
and the world unravelled.

The ridges rose: straight, high, silent.

They echoed thoughts
I hadn't known I carried—
unsaid, unnamed, yet deeply mine.

Behind me, caves yawned—
not carved by hands,
but shaped by centuries of listening.

Below, the mist curled
like forgotten dreams
trying to be remembered.

Silence pulsed—
like a drum just after being struck.

The cliff felt like an illusion—
real, yet trembling at the edges of belief.

The wind came in waves—
bursting, then vanishing—
as if remembering how to speak,
then forgetting again.

Time swayed in silence
echoes arrived before sound...
and known orders dissolved into myth.

A lone falcon circled the pale sky.
The mountains stood still,
witnessing each memory
that silence brought home.

The Sage: Ketu…

When I arrived,
he stood at the cliff's edge— arms open,
as if holding the horizon in embrace.
Barefoot, wrapped in wind, silence, and sky.
He was Ketu: the one who listens to stones.

His body was lean, sun-browned.
Hair tied back like river roots.
He looked carved by time, not aged.
His eyes—sharp, inward-lit like flint—
saw past what sight allows.
His ears, wide and sculpted by wind,
were made to hear what's never spoken.

His cave wasn't carved into the cliff.
It was remembered—
a chamber
where silence rested
like sacred fire folded in ash.

Ash-marked walls
bore no names—
only memory.
The air carried a scent—
minerals, fermented herbs, and
time left open.

He touched a hanging bell,
but didn't ring it.
"They called me mad," he said.

"But the stones... they know who kneels."

Once I reached, I felt bare.
The height unsettled me.
The sky unfolded above.
Vast, heavy, uncertain.
My thoughts tumbled
like loose stones down a slope.
I didn't know
if I could return.

Or if I even needed to.

"Do you know if mountains speak?"
I asked Ketu.

He didn't answer…
not at once.

His gaze
drifted toward the peaks.
Then he folded inward,
eyes closed,
listening with his whole being.
Then whispered, "They don't."
Then added, low and steady,
"What you hear is yours.
The mountain reflects what you bring.
Speak fear

—and fear returns.
Echoes don't lie. They reveal."

The next day,
he gave me a stone. It was flat, grey, and silent.
Asked me to hold.
"This stone has heard more prayers
than all the temples ever offered."

He pointed to the ledge.
"You sit there. Still. Silent.
Let your words fall like water.
When they return—
they'll be smaller. Clearer. True."

He gestured toward the ledge, where silence waited.
And asked me to sit and call—
not with words, but
with the raw weight of the truest feeling…
once each day.
Then wait.

He said, "No echo will return.
Until you are no longer trying."

So I called.

I called with despair.
With deep yearning.
I laughed in sudden ecstasy.

I wept with ache and grief.
I hurled everything I knew—
every named feeling,
every voice I had ever worn.

But the mountain stayed still.
The air swallowed it all.

Days passed.

Then one morning,
it opened my chest—
and something left me.
I didn't know what it was.
I didn't shape it.
I didn't name it.
It rose like breath let go—
pure, unheld.

And then,
it came back.
Not as echo but as laughter.

It was him, laughing.

That day, I understood—
an echo isn't repetition.
It is reflection.
Not of sound,
but of soul.

It was then I forgot
how to perform.
I stopped shaping feeling into form.
And I remembered how to feel—
raw, unresolved.
A prayer too honest for words.

I let the wind carry what was unnamed.
I let the river wash away what was heavy.
I let the light erase the need to know.

And the mountain—
he answered.

Not with sound,
but with stillness inside my chest.

The cliff never spoke.
But when I wept without armour,
the wind did not turn away.
It held me.

And he—
the voice within—
returned clearer than ever before.

That was clarity.
Not an answer.
But a presence.
And it was all I ever needed to hear.

All I would ever carry.

At dawn,
Ketu stood beside me.
The cliff held its breath.
Hushed before the sun.

He placed the black shard in my hand.

"This is next," he said.
"A cave with no mouth,
yet it breathes.
There waits one
who sees in the dark."

He turned toward the rising sun.
"Follow the smoke where no fire burns.
She lives inside the shadow."
Then he was gone.

The obsidian pulsed in my palm—warm, alive.
I descended.

Hours later, around a bend in the hill,
I saw smoke rising into the sky.
But no flame.

I stood again at the brink—
obsidian glowing faint.

Like an ember remembering fire.
My steps were no longer tentative.
The mountain didn't loom.
It listened.
I didn't speak.
There was no need for echo anymore.

From a hidden valley
a thread of smoke curled upward.
An invitation written in haze.

I closed my eyes.
I didn't retreat.
I readied myself to face what waited.

"I'm not the sound," I whispered.
"I'm the silence that gives it shape."

The mountain didn't reply.
It never had to.

Later, waking felt different.
Not that the world had changed
for me or against me—
but as if
everything had quietly rearranged around me.

I turned toward the smoke,
rising from no fire.
I walked into a cave with no mouth,

yet breathing—
like something half-remembered from a dream.

Behind me,
in the stone and silence,
a laugh lingered.

End of Passage Three.

4.2 The Ash That Listens.

I didn't see her at first.
Only the breath—faint, curling at the cave's mouth.
Stone still pressed its memory against my flesh.
like a second breath.
Smoke threaded through my hair.
Myrrh moved in my veins.
Time couldn't follow.
Then I heard it again.
Not a voice.
Not footfall.
Something older than sound moving inside silence.
And then—I saw her.
Rusha;
Waiting beneath a bent juniper,
tracing spirals on stone
with the char of something once burnt.
Smoke drifted behind her,
as if remembering the shape it used to wear.
"You came back," she said.
Not as greeting—
as knowing.

I knelt.
"You always leave. That's the only way you return," she smiled.
Small and endless.
I sat across from her.
My knees met the dust.
The cave's silence still echoed inside me,
like a question with no mouth.
"It didn't speak," I said. "Not in words.
Just silence."
"That's how the oldest truths arrive," she said,
drawing another circle.
"Not through noise. Through the skin."
She looked different that day—
tired and still.
The wind hadn't touched her hair.
There was dirt on her cheek.
She didn't wipe it away.
As if she were lost in memory.
"Were you in there?" I asked.
"Not quite. I was around it.
Smoke doesn't need to enter. It wraps."
"I wasn't afraid of getting lost," I said.
"I feared I'd dissolve into the silence."
"That's the beginning."
Her voice was low but intuitive. She continued,
"Of remembering who you are,"
She reached into a fold of her shawl,
pulling out a dried fig.
Warm. Soft. Crushed.
"Do you dream?"
"There's never quite enough time for sleep," she said.
A mischief glinting behind her stillness.

“Who carries your breath when you are elsewhere?”
"I wait inside someone’s silence."
I chewed slowly.
The fig was sweet. Hard. And sticky.
Like something dissolving beneath rain.
"Ketu said the mountain returns unknown inside."
"And what do you carry now?" she asked,
looking into me.
I opened my palm—
a piece of black stone.
"This," I said.
She touched my hand—
her fingertips brushed past—fleeting as memory on bone.
A spark passed through me.
"That’s what breathes in me now,"
she murmured—
her voice brushing my skin like dusk.
She didn’t move,
yet something within her stepped closer.
Her silence leaned into me—
without shape,
without distance.
It was drawing me into a memory
I hadn’t lived yet.
"How do you become aware of me?" she asked,
"By sound? Or by scent?"
She came close and whispered—
"With warmth," I replied.
"Then I have entered you,
Like a prayer folded into breath."
We didn’t speak after that.
I finished the fig.

The wind rose with a whisper,
carrying ash to the waiting trees.
When I stood, she was still drawing.
One circle inside the next.
No center. No edge.
I didn't ask when I'd see her again.
The silence had already answered.
She didn't look up,
but her hand reached toward mine—
thumb brushing soot along my wrist.

4.3 Summary: The Stone Listener.

The mountain did not echo words.
It answered the weight beneath them—
ache, presence, and whatever could not be said.
Up there, the silence was not emptiness.
It was a mirror where speech touched the shape of things without names.
Ketu did not teach by voice.
He taught by standing still—beside winds, beside breath—
Letting the mountain speak through what it returned.
Nothing echoed back. Only what had waited too long to be heard.
The cliff did not repeat. It revealed.
Held the struggle without asking.
And listening began.
Not as an act—but as an offering.
A shard remained. Obsidian.
The memory
where a voice stopped performing—
it became its pulse.
From stone to smoke.

From echo to hush.
From asking to warmth.
That was the turning—
not reaching outward, but folding inward.
And then Rusha returned.
She did not break the silence.
She *complimented* it—as a reflection.
She traced doubt with the gentleness of ash.
She did not resolve it—she let it breathe.
Her presence did not explain, it remembered.
When form trembled, she whispered—
"Form isn't fixed. Ash softens, warmth reshapes, touch remembers."
With her, philosophy became intimacy.
Listening grew tender.
And in memory, it learned how to breathe again.
She did not walk ahead or behind.
She waited— inside the pause
where becoming begins.
End of Chapter 4.

Chapter 5: The Cave of Smoke.

5.1 Passage Four – The Cave of Smoke.

There is darkness in all of us.
It does not shout—
it calls, slow and soft.
As if it has always known us.
But we turn away.
And in that turning, it carves us
into shapes we never meant to wear.
It never leaves.
It doesn't chase—
but it waits.
I wore the blindfold too long.
When I let it fall, the shadow stopped following.
What remained were fragments—
not of evil
but of what was never fully seen.
And when I stopped trying to avoid,
something deeper opened—
and quiet knowing beneath the noise.

I came down from the hills, following forgotten jungle trails.
Sometimes I rested beneath tree trunks,
letting the earth hold my weight.
Along the way,
I crossed a few villagers.
They startled me at first—
but without a word, they offered food and water.
No questions, no names exchanged.
Just kindness.

The path grew emptier, and I stopped counting time.
The days became unnamed.
Then, one evening, I saw it—
a thin thread of smoke
rising into the sky far off.
I followed it in silence.
Days folded into nights.
I kept walking.
Past exhaustion, past meaning.
And when the moon had long turned,
I came to a slit in the hill's gorge—
a narrow wound in stone,
waiting to be entered.

Inside, the cave was shadow-thick.
A single barely reached ground.
The air was moist and damp.
No birdsong entered.
As if sound itself paused at the threshold.
The stillness deepened with every step.
But it wasn't hollow. It was full—
of something ancient.
And watching—
not with eyes, but with knowing.
"I wasn't afraid.
The silence did not judge.
It remembered me—
not by shape or name,
but by who I was before language began.
Before memory had a form."
And somewhere inside that stillness, I stirred.
Not from sleep—
but from forgetting.

A door opened, quietly, inside my chest.
I closed my eyes.
And the veil lifted—
not from the world,
but from within.

Sometime later, I stood again—this time with full awareness.
The silence was complete, yet it felt alive.
Smoke rose gently from the earth's skin,
and the stones glowed—not with light,
but as if cradling the memory of fire.
The air held a kind of reverence,
not of danger,
but of being watched.
Not by eyes,
by something older than sight.
Something that remembered me
before I remembered myself.

Smoke rose from the earth's skin.
Beneath it, lava burned—slow, patient, alive.
Moths and beetles, pulled by heat at dusk.
They circled the fire with quiet devotion.
drawn into an unseen orbit.
Their movement carved delicate patterns,
as if they were writing an invisible hymn
in the smoky dusk.
And then, the veil lifted.
I remembered—
not with my mind,
but with something older inside me.

Some memories don't belong to this life, yet we carry them.
Not forgotten, only buried.

The Sage: Ravya:

Ravya sat in a corner of the furnace—
not speaking, not moving. Just being.
Stillness wrapped around her like breath.
A single ember danced beside her,
echoing the cave's quiet rhythm.
She didn't open her eyes.
She didn't need to.
"The world lies most when it shines,"
she whispered—
as if speaking to the stone,
or to the memory of fire itself.
She seemed elsewhere,
not lost in thought, but held by it.
When dawn came,
the ember dimmed.
Attachments dissolved like mist,
as if nothing ever clung at all.

I had grown quiet.
But it wasn't the kind of silence that frees.
It was guarded—layered with seams I couldn't close, or soften.
Stillness weighed heavy.
I held it, but it didn't hold me.
I didn't know how to let it melt.
Didn't know the way to dissolve

what lingered just beneath the hush.

One night, without turning, she spoke into the smoke.
"You must meet what you buried before you gave it names."
She pointed me to a brass bowl filled with water.
And asked me hold it in air.
The water inside trembled like a quiet breath.
"Stare," she said.
"Until you see the truth..."
Then I saw my own reflection in it—
an older, deeper one who were carrying stories untold.
Behind them, my mother's smile flickered,
soft and distant.
Tears welled up—not for her,
but for the pain that drifted, lost,
without direction or name.
The water trembled again.
Then she whispered,
"Smoke reveals what fire hides.
Look into the unclear."

She led me into a dark tunnel.
"Stay until you see," she said—without looking back.
And then she left, leaving me alone without food or fire.
In that blackness, time lost meaning.
Hunger vanished.
Fear softened into stillness.
The heavy air pressed close,
and dizziness pulled me down.
I fell asleep, surrendered to the dark.

When I woke, shapes moved around me—
not from the cave,
but from deep within myself.
Anger, guilt, and nameless shames,
all circling in the shadows.
I cried.
I whispered into the silence.
No answer came—
until I did.
A soft, forgiving voice inside me,
breaking the darkness with quiet mercy.

In the absence of light,
things showed their truest shape.
I saw them—
and did not turn away.
I opened my eyes.
But when I blinked,
I realized they had never closed.
Shapes shifted within the dark,
clear and unhidden.
She touched my shoulder.
"Now," she said, "you understand.
Fire was never the enemy.
You entered its center.
Your vision held—
not because you fought,
but because you stopped running.
What opens in truth
cannot be burned again."

I had no lamp in that cave.
Yet I saw—

a self-unfinished—boy, son, ember, and echo.
All of them were me.
Those were not only the sheds I was carrying,
but also who I dared to be.
Because that day, without a lamp,
I had to become the light itself.

When I was ready to leave,
she pressed a vial into my hand.
"For the place where flame returns to the surface," she said.
"When it begins to burn your feet, pour it—and wait."
Then, with ash, she drew a spiral on my palm.
It was no mere symbol.
"Follow it," she whispered.
"Fire bows to those who've faced their own darkness."
She didn't say goodbye.
She simply turned and walked away.
That day, she inscribed a memory.
I stepped out of the cave.
The earth embraced me—
and I felt it, anew.

The cave closed its door behind me.
The earth was warm beneath my feet.
Rusha was waiting—silent—by the riverbed.
End of Passage Four.

5.2 The Fire That Does Not Burn.

The ground still held its heat
like a secret too old to let the world know.
The riverbed was almost dry.

The silence made them forget their course.
I walked through it towards her.
Rusha was waiting at a place
where the river had once run.
Her clothes were worn.
Seeing me coming, she softened
into a quiet permission, I noticed.
"You went inside the smoky cave,"
she asked in a feeble voice.
"I thought I was going to lose sight," I told her. "Instead,
it opened up a secret into a shape."
She noded.
I sat beside her.
I took rest for a while.
Later, I said,
"I forgot my name."
She smiled, and I didn't understand why.
Then she said, "Finally,"
as if relieved of something important.
A sudden burst of wind swept through.
Ash rose into the air.
Strands of her hair lifted with it.
She took out rock salt and jaggery
from banana bark—soft and clean—
and offered them to me.
I felt grace given, not earned.
I ate them immediately.
"I've been waiting here for nights," she said.
"And this water did not flow.
But I knew you would."
"Why did you wait?" I asked, longing in my voice.

Instead of answering,
she looked toward the horizon.
Red flickers began to glow.
"Because fire doesn't need a mirror," she said after a pause.
"It looks for what hides behind them."
"Does fire purify?" I asked her.
"No," she replied softly.
"It reminds us of sacrifice.
And asks us to choose."
She drew shapes in the dust,
and the wind erased them.
"No! I don't want to," I murmured.
"Then give yourself," she said gently.
"And nothing will burn you again."
She leaned in and held my hand.
"Fire is waiting for you," she said.
"It does not chase but asks for your invitation."
"And what if I don't invite it?" I asked.
"I will wait again.
From the other side."
I closed my eyes at her words.
I didn't try to hold her presence—
I let it pass through me,
like something that won't stay,
but won't leave either.
Without a word, she stood.
Her shadow fell on me.
"You are not alone.
You never were."
She walked toward the edge of the riverbed—
not away from me.

And I felt the unknowing begin to dissolve.

5.3 Summary: The Cave of Smoke.

Some truths don't speak. They wait in silence.
The cave offered no answers.
It returned Dhruv to the part of himself
that remembered before memory began.
Ravya never questioned him.
She gave him the dark—not to frighten,
but to let "what was buried" rise within.
And then, Dhruv finally listened.
In that blackness, his voice returned—
quieter, older.
He hadn't closed his eyes.
He stopped looking.
The smoke didn't blind him.
It revealed. Gently. Steadily.
As though he had stopped running
from what he already knew was his name.
He did not come out clean.
He emerged clearer—
not whole, but unhidden.
When Rusha met him again,
she didn't ask who he'd become.
She only said, "Finally."
She knew what he realized.
Inner light, when welcomed, reveals
what is hidden deep inside and asks us to face it to dissolve.
It reveals what is truly ours.
So Dhruv walked forward,
not because he was ready,

but because he had already walked
through what he feared most.
What remained was not to conquer flame,
but to stand inside it—
unhidden.

End of Chapter 5.

Chapter 6: The One Who Burns.

6.1 Passage Five – The One Who Burns.

I had seen my shadow.
Now, I had to become light.
But light never arrives clean.
I must pass the test.
It will burn attachments and self-beliefs.
This fire invites.
I wasn't afraid of pain.
I feared what would remain
after there was nothing left to burn.

The soil was cracked like an old wound, and water was memory.
I chewed bitter roots, their juice stinging but enough to feed myself.
I saw no village—only a few shepherds in the distance.
I carried no hopes, and they met me with nothing but an unfamiliar quiet.
At night, smoke rose from the hills,
carrying a pungent burning smell.
Red flickering fires danced across the slopes.
I understood I had reached my destination—
an invitation wrapped in a warning.

I did not fear. That had already burned away.
I was ready.
The smoke I once survived now lives inside me.
I was not brave, either— it was inevitable.
The fire does not ask.
And I knew there was no pause.

A black earth stretched across a wide circular field.
Fissures hissed with a breath too hot to be air.
At the center, yellowish sulfur coiled into pillars.
Molten lava waited to burst.
And at the heart, a patch of scorched yet unburnt grass remained.
The heat holds its breath—for absence.

Flames rose. The hot stones fumed.
It looked like the Earth's rage.
But it was not.
It was neither god nor wrath.
This was the fire remembering its name.

The Sage: Agniya:
Agniya stood at the center.
Barefoot, wearing only a piece of red cloth,
wrapped around his hips.
His eyes were sharp and silent—
compact and scarred.
His skin held the memory of fire—and resolve.
Everything about him was deliberate and exact.

I approached him.
My mouth was dry, skin cracked, jaw slackened.
But I didn't kneel.
I stood tall—
at least, I tried.
Not in defiance,
but in surrender.
He said, "You came to die."
I said nothing.

He nodded.
"Good. Then let it be."

I sat beside the burning bed.
And ate with him: burned root and hot water
On the third day,
he gave me a glowing ember
and asked me to hold it tight.
"Name those unnecessary parts inside you," he said.
"Then burn them."
I was ready.
I named them all.
And a shift happened inside me.
I felt lighter—relieved.
I looked at him
and said, "I have burned it all. I burned my name."
His eyes brightened.
"Then let it go.
People wear many selves.
To become the truer self, one must shed all others."

He handed me a clay vessel filled with oil.
"Do not spill a drop," he warned.
I walked across the scorched field,
the ground still warm beneath my feet.
Each step demanded more awareness than I'd ever
known.
But the vessel cracked and oil spilled all over the earth.
He struck the ground once—
flames rose.
"You learn from your mistakes," he said,
"if you're willing to face them fully."

Last night, I stepped into the ring.
The grass beneath me blackened,
yet pulsed—alive.
Flames leapt around, but did not strike—
they held their fire without destruction.
I stood still.
Because I knew,
The one who has burned from within
cannot burn again.

Fire revealed—it didn't destroy.
It cut clean—it didn't consume.
What remained was true.
I stood at the center.
And the flames quieted before the truth I no longer denied.

The next morning,
Agniya handed me a red stone.
It felt cool in my palm.
"Keep it close," he said, "you'll need it."
Then he pointed northward.
"You are ready. Go now.
You will find the glacier—
hidden in a high mountain valley to the north."

When I returned,
I carried the fire within.
I was not exhausted.
From a distance, I saw Rusha waiting.
I sensed she had seen the trials I had faced in Agniya's flame.
And I had no questions left.

She remained silent, watching me
As if watching me fall apart was the only way she
believed I'd return complete.
I stepped toward her,
yearning to hear her thoughts.
But when I blinked, she was gone—
vanished without a trace.
End of Passage Five.

6.2 The Cold That Remembers.

I walked for days.
Snowfall began—not like music,
but like a merciless ghost—
silent, cold, unsentimental.
That night, I sheltered beneath a rock nose.
My shawl tore, then stiffened from the cold.
I didn't speak for days.
The apricots, the shepherds had given me
hardened in my pouch.
At some point,
the wind lost its sharpness,
and the cold became part of me.
Then Rusha came.
She arrived like a thought —
quietly, when the earth paused.
A white robe wrapped around her; her hair held high by
a wooden pin.
She exhaled; the warmth drifted—
into the air, vanishing into the snow.
Rusha looked at me for a moment.
"You're thinner than before," she said,
her voice soft but unpitying.

"Something heavy is gone," I replied.
"I feel clear."
"The cold permits only what's honest to remain," she said.
"Maybe that's how it should be."
She sat beside me.
I thought of mentioning the dry field—
how she'd disappeared—but the moment passed.
Snow clung to her like silence, and she didn't brush it off.
"Did the fire take everything from you?" she laughed.

I let the silence reply.
But I remembered —
she once said she would ask what remains.
And now she had.
After a few moments of pause, I broke the truth,
said, "Yes. And then the cold came to see what remained."
She watched the embers struggle to take shape.
"And what did it find?" she asked.
I turned toward her.

"A boy who remembers the warmth of being held,
but doesn't need it anymore."
She closed her eyes.
There was nothing to give,
only her presence and the truth of staying.
"I always come after the trials. Don't I?
Want to know why?" she asked.
"Because I wouldn't hear you otherwise."

"No," she whispered.
"Because you wouldn't see, otherwise —
what I bring. Not until now."
I reached for Vahu's shell inside my satchel and pressed it to my ear.
No hum, no echo.
"Even this is quiet now."
"It is waiting. It will speak when there is a need," she said.
"Some love isn't spoken."
Her pause let the snow speak in the stillness between us.
I felt the cold in my bones and tried not to freeze.
"You said you want to let the fire in," I murmured.
"You are right. But the cold didn't care.
It entered," she smiled—
not with joy, but with recognition.
"The cold freezes anything soft."
"Everything is memory. It remembers the origin. Even the ice is," I said.
She was quiet, but glowing with a fullness—
that I never want to read.
She came closer and let her head fall to my shoulder—
quietly, like trust.
"Hope you're not going to dissolve like ice," she whispered.
"You are the shield that is forming."
A glimpse of hope fired up inside me.
She pulled back.
"Next, you meet the stillness."
I didn't hold back.
"Will you wait for me there?"

Her footprints faded in the snow as she watched them.
"No. I'll arrive after. I'll ask you what you could not see there."
She stood.
I was silent. I didn't look back,
but breathed deeply.
Her footprints disappeared into the snow.
She was already gone.

6.3 Summary: The One Who Burns.

Some trials sear. Others wait.
The fire burned away the excess.
The cold did not freeze; it revealed what survived.
Even speech faded, and need dimmed.
Dhruv sat alone, with faith that silence had become his language.
Then Rusha came. She wore white.
She didn't speak of fire.
The cold entered silently and found the soft places.
But Dhruv knew he could endure.
That knowing was his strength.
She did not answer the silence.
She sat within it.
She arrived after the trials.
She was not a balm, but a reflection.
Her final words lingered:
Not all lessons blaze.
Some arrive in what survives.
The cold reminds us of those fire forgets.
End of Chapter 6.

Chapter 7: The Glacier of the Still Time.

7.1 Passage Six – The Glacier of the Still Time.

Narrator:

> We often mistake stillness for silence. But they are not the same. The pause between two events isn't just quiet silence—it holds something deeper. In that moment, we do not merely stop; we descend inward. We feel what unfolded. We feel what is waiting. We see what is hidden. And then, we speak again.
>
> This stillness, once, became my companion.
>
> In my younger days, I stood at the edge of a frozen lake. I've long forgotten the name or the path—but not the feeling. There were no ripples, no rustle, not even movement. Only a divine presence.
>
> The pause between two breaths grew wide enough to become a world. Still yet fully living.
>
> In that stillness, silence inscribed something no words could reach.

So I arrived in the north, at the glacier,
after walking through fire.
They say time melts everything up here.
But here, nothing melted.
I had stepped into a realm
where memory remained frozen,
where time had stopped turning.
And in that stillness, I did not walk forward.
I vanished.
Not from fear.

But as an offering to peace.

I moved slowly.
The air thinned. And the quiet deepened.
I took shelter in caves.
A hush of sacredness lingered there—
like the residue of old prayers.
I imagined monks had once sat here,
breathed stillness into the stone.
By day, the snow felt like a blessing.
By night, it changed.
The cold crept in like a thought
that wouldn't leave.
The silence held its breath.
A pair of goats stood nearby, watching.
Then, without sound, they vanished.
That night, I found two shepherds huddled near a low fire.
Their skin was cracked from the weathered wind.
Their faces were unreadable.
We said nothing.
They gave what little they had:
a few dried apricots,
a thin blanket,
and room beside their fire.
Their silence wasn't empty.
It was worn.
Like something they had carried too long.
In the morning, as I rose to leave,
one of them looked at me.
A stillness passed between us.
And said, "Silence that kills not cold."

I said nothing.
But I remembered his words.
Like a glow that stayed long after the fire had gone.

Since the field of fire, every step had been a sharp climb upward.
The trees had thinned. The forest had turned back—
as if they forgot their home.
The fire within me had stilled.
Even the blood moved slower now.
It too had surrendered to the cold.
My walk became more like a drift.
There was no urgency left in my limbs,
no command to give them.
The cold didn't invade.
It entered gently, like a guest I could not refuse.
I let it settle. I let it stay.
And in that silence,
I began to long—not for survival,
but for a slow and peaceful dissolution.

It lay between the ridges
like a slumbering god—vast, ancient, and breathing.
Its body shimmered
with blue-white light,
veined with frozen secrets.
There were fractures across its surface,
as if it had once spoken—
then fallen silent.
The silence here wasn't absence.
A presence. Immense...
Every sound I made returned to me—
softened, altered—

as if it had passed through memory
before reaching back.
I exhaled.
My breath turned to frost and lingered mid-air,
it was reluctant to disappear.

The sky was burned blue.
The air struck raw—like flint sparking inside the chest.
No birds called.
Even the sun moved here with caution.
The world had stilled in a breath—
caught between inhale and surrender.
I stepped into that prayer.

The Sage: Himya.

She waited in an alcove of ice—
wrapped in wool and silence.
She was Himya: *inner frost*.
Her hair fell like snowfall.
Her face bore no mark of time.
She didn't blink.
And when her voice came,
it moved like a thought through bone.
She had once ruled, once commanded.
Then one day, she walked north—
until the thoughts stopped chasing her,
and stayed behind.
Her presence was like snow—cold and unmoved,
but never cruel.

I arrived empty—
with only a whisper of fire left inside.

The questions I carried
grew heavier in the silence.
I longed to lie down in the snow
and surrender.
But then I saw her—
still as the ancient hills.
And it struck me—I hadn't come to fade away.
I had come to learn.
To witness the way silence is conquered.

Why does pain return, again and again?" I asked, softly.
She looked through me.
"You do not stay with it
long enough to let it go."
"I'm tired of seeking," I admitted.
"Then be still," she said.
"The glacier does not seek the sky.
The sky finds it."
One morning, without a word,
she laid a shard of ice in my palm.
"This is time," she said.
"Transparent. Still. And cold.
And yet—
it changes everything."
"Watch it," she whispered.
"And do nothing."

She walked me to a stretch of frozen earth.
Above—only sky.
Then she said, "Stay here till morning.
Do not move. No fire survives here,
except the one within."
And she left.

I sat.
The wind spoke what suffering could not name.
My body resisted.
Cold chewed through flesh,
bit at bone.
Time thinned like a thread on the verge of snapping—
I surrendered.
The cold outside met the cold within.
Stillness arrived.
And all dissolved.
By morning,
I was no longer trembling.
I was listening.

When the sun returned,
I wept—not from sorrow,
but release.
Time had melted into silence.
And in that stillness,
I found myself again—
not the one who arrived,
but the one who remained.
The watcher.
The survivor.
The one without a name.
Yet never lost.

I sat at the edge and waited.
It did not demand or rush.
Time, now a fading breath,
dissolved into the cold.
But the cold didn't freeze me—
it stripped, softened, and cleared.

And when it passed through me, I remained.
Not untouched, but unveiled.
I had not burned. I had not shattered.
I was simply—new.

Before I left, Himya handed me a black feather,
frozen inside a small cube of ice.
Her fingers trembled as she held it out.
"When this melts," she said,
"follow the shadow that flies.
It will take you where
you must forget everything—
even your name."

The glacier fell away behind me.
But the silence followed—
like a breath that had learned to wait.
So did she.
She lingered in the hush between questions.
Time fell quiet within me.
In that stillness, I found the watcher within.
I was no longer seeking truth or wisdom,
but ready now for a softer mirror—
one that spoke in the ache of remembering someone dear.
This was a new kind of hush.
Not of ice, but of intimacy.
And so I left the glacier.
But the silence came with me.
It stayed, not as weight, but as witness.
I was ready.
To begin the next passage.
End of Passage Six.

7.2 Where Names Fade.

Narrator:

> On his way down from the glacier, silence stayed beside him.
> His feet were torn. His breath shallowed. But he walked lighter.
> Neither pain nor fear of it held him now. He took shelter inside a ruined shrine.
> There, he listened to the wind arguing with tattered prayer flags.

I was coming down from the mountain.
I took refuge in a ruined shrine that night.
A faint sound stirred—not an echo.
It answered me.
Then I saw Rusha.
Her hair was unbound.
Her eye—deep.
She moved as if the moonlight had poured itself into her.
"You remembered me," she said.
Her voice was soft, like a breeze.
"Even while forgetting yourself."
She smiled.
I whispered,
"Yes. I remembered you. I don't remember anything else."
I gripped the corner of the *swal*.
But I did not rise. Or could not.
In a quiet corner, she brushed away the ash clinging to her clothes.
"You've reached here, haven't you?" she asked.
"It is not a place," I said.
"Not even a thought. It is... absence.
Full and complete."

She was playing with a stone,
a smile curled on her lips.
"That's where I live," she said.
"And that place—
you won't need it anymore."
I looked up at her.
I didn't understand what she said.
"I lost my name," I said.
"The cold had frozen it into ice—then it was gone forever."
"Nothing happens unnecessarily," she said,
her gaze unwavering.
"It means—it has begun for you."
I tried to sit up.
The charcoal floor whispered back into silence.
But her warmth held me there.
"I once believed you were nothing more than a shadow of memory," I whispered.
"A grief made visible."
"You might have been right," she said,
tilting her head gently toward me.
"But now... you've earned me."
I looked at her—
the way someone does who's lost their story,
and chosen not to chase it.
"Will you leave me again?" I asked.
My voice barely a breath.
"If you anchor," she replied,
"I won't be held. But I will witness."
She stood.
Snow and moonlight gathered around her like an aura.

"Dhruv is a name given to you," she said,
not turning back.
"But love— was yours long before you ever existed."
"Then what should I call you?" I asked.
She stepped close. Met my eyes.
"You already do—
when you remember, even without speaking."
Then she stepped outside.
The moonlight received her—
The night opened into vastness.
She left, only a hush remained.
Alone in the ruin, I did not feel sorrow.
A tear rolled down my cheek.
I didn't know whether it was from recognition—
or something deeper. I didn't wipe it away.
That night, I slept. No dreams. No fear.
And no echo of my name.
It rested. Forever.

7.3 Summary: The Glacier of the Still Time.

It was a glacier, a place so still, even time could not escape.
From the furnace of silence, Dhruv's journey was shaped.
And then, he entered the glacier's hush—
a silence so vast that thought slowed,
emotion faded, and memory broke into shards.
There, he met Himya.
She did not teach. She *undid.*
She dissolved the very need to seek.
In her presence, even time learned to wait.
Dhruv learned simple being.
Not to move. Not to reach.

But to endure, without asking.
But here—explanations melted away.
What began as a physical challenge
became a sacred art—
Stillness.
Pain gave way to presence.
Movement to surrender.
Dhruv shed the weight of ego
and learned the quiet grace
of living in the present.
Yet, the journey did not end in stillness.
As he descended, something stirred.
The present returned to him—
in the form of Rusha,
who stepped into his silence
She was not his past.
She was his absence, made visible. The witness.
In her, Dhruv saw a truth.
Identity is not destroyed.
It simply no longer binds.
When one realizes identity is immortal,
then name, ego, and form become burdens.
Without those three,
a deeper presence awakens.
One that does not echo—
but *waits*.
One that does not speak—
but *is spoken through*.
This is the transformation.
The return, refined.
The coming back without clinging.
Dhruv—once lit by fire,
once summoned by name—

now sits in a quiet corner.
He no longer asks. But he hears.
The universe finds those who no longer seek.
And in its hush, he falls asleep—
the kind of sleep that does not echo a name.
It simply holds. Like peace.
End of Chapter 7.

Chapter 8: The Temple of Forgetting.

8.1 Passage Seven – The Temple of Forgetting.

It is a place where life unfolds beyond knowing.
Memory loses shape.
Language dissolves.

A spiralled path led me to the temple.
There, silence had taken form—
a quiet soul waiting for me.

Peace didn't fall around me.
It settled within, as stillness.

I felt forgetting not as a wound.
A release.

All the stories I had once counted,
the voices I had clung to,
the wounds I had tracked—
all faded,
like music remembered in sleep.

I dissolved into that hush—
not as a seeker,
but as something silence might one day remember.

The descent from the glacier was steep—
and dreamlike.

Ice cracked beneath my feet.
Each step fractured some old certainty.

Shrines rose from the stone—
stacked by hands long gone.

Colorful prayer flags fluttered,
symbols of forgotten wishes,
faded into wind.

Nights turned hollow.
I slept in wind-bitten caves,
limbs aching,
thoughts thickened with echoes.

I survived on barley rotis, dried apricots,
and snowmelt cupped in my palm.

I wasn't the boy who had left—
but I wasn't someone new either.

My mind carried too many stories,
tangled and overgrown like wild vines.

Even the dreams had grown restless,
looping, repeating,
losing shape in their own weight.

I didn't need more stories.
Not rest.

But a clearing.

The temple was broken.
And quiet.

Moss had swallowed its bones.
The roots claimed the stone,
as though the forest had sworn never to let go.

Inside, the hall stretched wide.
The chamber curved inward.

Echoes moved like secrets.
The walls held the hush of ancient trees—
as though tracing the memory of prayer.

Silver chimes stirred softly.
The wind returned to greet the unspoken.

The air held a fragrance—
of bark, of incense,
hovering where the material touches the unseen.

It was a place where silence waited.
Where the temple, though broken, still breathed.

I didn't speak.
Even thought felt like an intrusion.

It was a place at the edge of something old,
not a ruin,
but a presence withdrawn into stillness.

The stones remembered without voice.
And my memory began to fade.

Pale mist clung to the air—
like a thought only half-formed.

Somewhere, hidden,
a ripple sounded.
Its echo lingered inside the silence.

The stream itself remained unseen.

Shadows drifted along the stone walls,
moving with the slowness of breath withheld.

The air was cool and moist,
carrying the scent of damp earth.
It settled over everything—
not heavy, but certain.

Here, nothing declared itself.
Time had forgotten how to count.
And even sound had lost its way.

The Sage: Smriti.

Her hair shimmered like moonlit frost.
Her presence was faint, almost translucent—
like a breath paused inside stone walls.

She didn't speak much.
Even the sound of my breath
felt louder than her voice.

She wore silence.
Her robe was stitched with dry leaves,
trailing the scent of ash and age.

Once, she carried names.
Once, lifetimes bowed to her.
Whispers used to follow her like wind.
But its weight broke her.

She came here—
not to worship,
but to be unburdened.

The temple was no shrine,
but a refuge.

Scrolls lay across the floor,
dust-laden, brittle, unread.

She never reached for them.
Never once read.

"A temple is a place to release," she said.

And in the stillness between her breaths,
I felt the weight
of all I had forgotten
to forget.

I didn't arrive here with strength.
I arrived with a voice
that had finally learned how to stay.

Thoughts pressed in—
crowded and thick,
like robes worn layer over layer,
too heavy for warmth.

I didn't come to understand them.
I didn't want to.
I came here to let them go.

Every story.
Every echo.
Every name.

To leave each piece of it in the hush
that asks for nothing back.

"Why must we forget?" I asked.
"Memory is sacred. Isn't it?"

"Yes," she said softly.
"So is space."

Her gaze rested on the moving shadows
along the temple wall.

Then she turned to me.
"You tell me—
what grows in a forest
where no light enters?"

She paused.

"Some memories are blessings.
Others are like borrowed robes—
beautiful, but heavy.

Grief. Guilt.
The name you were handed,
not the one you became.

Too many to name."

She leaned closer.
"You must remember who you are.
But just as importantly—
you must forget who you are not."

Then she asked—
"Take each name.

Each wound.
Each sorrow you've carried like breath."

And release them
into the hollow heart of the temple.

So I did.

For days, I stayed.

I whispered.
I laughed, once.
I wept like rain remembered.
And offered confessions rose from the still, aching depth of pain.

I spoke until there was nothing left
but silence.

And even that,
I gave away.

On the fourth day, I arrived.

Not hollow—
not as I had feared.

But something had emptied.

The ache.
The quiet hunger of attachment.

They slipped from me
into the stillness of the temple,
like breath released in sleep.

The need to carry those memories was gone.
They were never mine to keep.

And with their leaving,
the burden of needing anything at all vanished too.

My heart, once crowded, opened.
And the light, unasked and quiet, passed through me.

I left a name on every stone.
A sorrow in every echo.

And when it slipped from my mouth,
I did not disappear.

I became space.
Became sky.
Became a field—wide and open,
where what has yet to arrive might one day belong.

As I turned to leave,
Smriti handed me a shard of mirror.

"You're here not to seek," she said softly
"Not as a child."

Her voice was low, steady.

"But as a mirror—
not to reflect, but to forget."

Then, leaning closer, she whispered:
"Go where the light cannot reach—the cave that holds the dark
Something ancient waits there—
You will not remember it.
You must rediscover it… through the act of forgetting."

As memories grew quiet
and attachments began to fall away,
I learned to see things in their truth.

Even my name felt like a burden
I no longer needed to carry.

And with that, the presence returned to me.

When silence becomes truer than remembering,
love arrives—
not as a story from the past,
but as something felt for the first time

End of Passage Seven.

8.2 The Cave Between Us.

I had almost forgotten she would return.
Or perhaps because she was no longer something to seek—
she had become part of my silence.

I reached the forest downhill.
The sky, once alive, now hung in stillness.

I saw Rusha standing at the opening of the temple gate.
It opened on the hillside
like a long wound breathing an ancient hush.

She was barefoot,
her toes brushing the rivulet
that traced down from the rocks.

Her fingers dipped into the flow—slow and silver.

Her hair hung loose, streaked with dust and dusk,
as if the day had laid its secrets across her crown.
A fallen leaf clung to her shoulder.

Her gaze met mine—
not with surprise,
but with the calm recognition
of something inevitable.

"You are thin," she said.

"Yes. But I didn't drop them," I replied, stepping closer.
"They dissolved. Names. Faces. Even the grief."

"And do you miss them?" she asked,
smiling gently, her head tilted.

I breathed.
The air here was thicker, fuller—almost tactile.

"Not yet," I said. "I will later.
Or I'll forget what missing feels like, too."

She didn't answer.
The silence between us stretched—soft, vast, alive.

Then she took a step back,
her shadow folded into the mouth of the cave.

"You're not coming in?" I asked.

Her eyes did not waver.
"I live outside your reflections—"
"What you find inside—you must meet alone."

The air tightened between us,
like a thread drawn through flesh—

I looked down...
touched the stone beside me.

The cave wall was cold and wet.
It felt ancient.
Moss gowned the crevices.

Water droplets stood still along the grain.
I imagined the mountain listening.

"It feels like the world is silent," I murmured.

She looked at me.
"Because you have," she said.
"And now… something must be exhaled."

I held her gaze.
My throat tightened.

"Why do you always return after I break?"

She stepped a little closer.
"Because only then are you whole enough to hold me."

I almost reached for her hand.
…But didn't.
I turned and stepped into the cave.

Behind me, her presence did not vanish.
Inside, the dark curved downward
I walked deeper.
Not toward silence—
but toward a self I could not name.
A memory too sacred for words.

8.3 Summary: The Temple of Forgetting.

Dhruv stepped into a temple not built for worship, but for unravelling.

There were no idols. No chants. No names carved in stone.
Only quiet. Only stillness.

Here, faith wasn't something to carry. It was something to lay down.

At the center sat Smriti— a seer, not for what she remembered,
but for what she let go.

She released without resistance.
Memory bowed itself out— like petals falling into water with no name.

She asked Dhruv to name each burden, each sorrow, each shape of self—
and release it.

This was not forgetting by force, but forgetting as grace.
Not erasure, but the quiet creation of space.

And Dhruv, instead of being diminished, was widened.

Then Rusha returned— not to rejoin his story, but to become its resonance.

She didn't guide. Didn't question. She stood outside the breath of the cave—
stillness made visible.

Only in that hush can true presence be met.

So Dhruv crossed another threshold—
into the question that arrives only after all remembering has dissolved.

He did not speak.
He became silence
that waits when every name has fallen away.

End of Chapter 8.

Chapter 9: The Cave of Echoes.

9.1 Passage Eight – The Cave of Echoes.

Speaking shapes the world—
but it's not the only truth.
Silence shapes it too.
In stillness, it replies.

It was such a place—
deep in the spine of the mountain,
where the air holds its breath.
There, I found the well's quiet mouth—
it gave back
not reflection,
but response.

I released many whispers.
Each one returned,
older, quieter—
as if belonging to someone
who remembered more than I ever knew.

The echoes weren't mine.
They were the mountain's memories,
awakened.

Here, to ask
is not to seek an answer.
It is to awaken a truth

too still for words,
too honest for noise.

I realized—
I had been too loud to listen.

I passed through mountain villages—
where the air smelled of pine sap,
rising slow,
as if time had roots.

The villagers gave me salt, coarse bread,
and a nod that meant
"We've all been there."

An old man handed me a blanket
and a piece of memory—
silent, folded, meant to be carried in cold.

At night,
the cold didn't threaten.
It passed cleanly,
like flint striking bone.
The warmth lingered—
not in the fire,
but in memory's frayed corners.

The cliffs grew narrow.
The trees thinned.
The soil deepened—ember red,

like something once burned
but still not done.

Even the wind fell silent.

Then I saw it.
The cave.
Not carved.
Not shaped.
Torn—like a wound left open,
not to speak, but to receive.

I carried no names.
They had long slipped from me—
like petals from a branch
no longer reaching for spring.

I had only one companion: my breath—
and the quiet thrum beneath it,
steady as a forgotten prayer.

I wasn't seeking.
I was listening—
to the hush behind my pulse,
where sound forgets language
and becomes permission.

Something long-buried stirred.
Not fully awake,

but turning gently toward the air.

The cave opened like a wound—raw, unfinished.
Ash lifted gently from the stone's hush.
Moss touched the threshold
like it remembered every foot that had passed before.

Inside, the path coiled inward—
a spiral, like a question left unanswered,
curving not toward meaning
but toward the place
where meaning unravels.

Each step I took was followed.
Not by echo. Not by shadow.

Something was responding.
Something that remembered me before I did.

The air thickened as I moved inward—
Stalactites hung like frozen tongues—
mid-prayer, forgotten.
Words had stopped before they ever found a voice.

Moss glowed along the walls,
soft and green, like thoughts that hadn't fully arrived.
Everything felt paused.
As if even time had set down its burden.

At the center of it all,
a patch of darkness curled in on itself.

It was not empty.
It pulsed.
Not with absence—
but with presence,
too vast to name.

The Sage: Nirvak.

He did not speak.
Ash veiled his cheekbones.
His chest, bare—etched like a flame that had forgotten to burn.

He sat on an obsidian slab, unmoving.
But his gaze peeled through thought,
like bark stripped from greenwood—
slow, knowing, without haste.

I called him Nirvak—
the one beyond words.

I thought I had nothing left hidden.
But the cave unearthed what even silence hadn't told me.

Voices rose—
ones I had buried without knowing when, or why.

They moved like shadows
from a past I never named.

It wasn't the darkness I feared.
It was the thought that darkness might love
what lives in me.

And in that moment,
I knew—
this was the self
I hadn't yet dared to welcome.

My voice returned.
But it was no longer mine.
It came back stripped—
echoing from a place I'd never been,
as if shaped by another life.

"Who am I?" I asked.
"Who do you believe?" the cave replied.

"I am nothing," I whispered.
"Then who is speaking?" it asked.

There was no judgment.
No command.
Only the hush of words returning
not as answers—
but as mirrors.

And in that silence,
I was handed back to myself.

Nirvak told me to sit in the cave's deepest dark.
Alone.
No fire. No food. No promise.
Only silence.

"Wait," he said, "until you hear an echo that is not your own."

So I waited.
I spoke. I wept. I sang broken songs into the stone.
Each sound returned the same. Familiar. Mine.
Days passed.
I licked salt from the walls.
Drank water seeping from stone like memory.
My voice thinned.
My body thinned.
But my mind grew wide and still.

Then one night—
the echo changed. It spoke back.

Not as a reflection,
but as a remembering.

The voice wasn't mine.
It was older.
It was deeper.

Something that had waited
across lifetimes to be heard again.

I broke.
Not from pain.
But from recognition.

I wept,
not to fill the silence—
but to honor what had finally returned.

It passed through Nirvak—
not as speech,
but as silence shaped by lifetimes.

He did not speak.
He held it.
Like stone holds water beneath
a thousand years of drought.

He remained still.
And the old ones rose—
not with sound,
but with weight,
with knowing.

I did not cry for him.
I cried because
the earth remembered
its voice.

And for the first time,
it wept
through me.

In the cave's core,
a voice found me—
older than language,
older than even the ache to ask.

It knew me
before belief had bones,
before longing had shape.

It didn't explain.
It didn't answer.
It simply called—
like memory from a time
before time.

And I wept.
Not for pain.
But for the home
I had forgotten
I missed.

I gathered myself—
not in strength,
but in a quiet steadiness.

Then Nirvak reached out
and placed something in my palm:
a shard of pottery,
etched with a spiral.
As if the wind had once whispered
its path into the clay.

I bowed in gratitude.
He remained in silence.

And from somewhere within me,
my voice rose and spoke:
"Climb to where breath becomes word.
And meet the one who says nothing—
but cannot lie."

I left Nirvak.
The cave folded into stillness behind me.
And I stepped into a hush
quiet enough to hold every self I ever had.

The sky hung above—vast, unblinking.
But I felt him within,
like a seed, the dark had warmed.

At the cave's mouth,
where silence had taken root,
she stood. Waiting.

No words.
No gesture.
Only presence—
That made language fall asleep.

End of Passage Eight.

9.2 The Sky between Words.

I climbed beyond forest, beyond moss,
until the mountain became sky—
wearing stone.

That's where the cliff forgot gravity.
Rusha waited there—
seated at the edge
as if it were the place she'd once been whole.
A gray shawl wrapped her.
Her braid lay quiet across her shoulder.
"You're late," she said, not turning.

"You're early."

"One of us had to wait." She shrugged.
"The sky's not great at small talk."

We sat.
Close enough for the silence to soften between us

Below us was the cliff.
Above—light.
Not sun.

Not moon.
Just light that hadn't yet chosen a form.

"This place doesn't pretend.
It doesn't need to," she said.
Her lips curved around a question she didn't ask.

I asked if she lies.
"Only when someone wishes it."

"Do I?"

"You don't need it anymore."

We stayed.
Not speaking.
But not silent either.

I whispered,
"Sometimes I wonder if I'm still walking…
or being walked."

She smiled.
"Will is a visitor.
But surrender?
That's how the mountain remembers you."

She placed a stone between us.
Etched with a spiral.
"It was mine. Then it wasn't.
Now it's yours—till it forgets."

"You know," I said,
"you come when I no longer seek you."

"Because needing is loud," she said.
"I speak where it's quiet."

I touched her—
in the way light touches and leaves.
Not fully. But felt.

"Would you save me if I fall?"

She smiled.
"Never. But I'd jump too."

Above us, a lone vulture circled.
Below, a feather drifted.
Neither rushed.
Both descending.

"Everything descends," she said.
"But not everything breaks."

"You're not real, are you?"

She looked straight through me.
"I'm as real as what remains
when everything else is stripped away."

That night, we didn't speak again.
But something passed between us—
not breath,

not thought.
Something like recognition.

When I closed my eyes,
I didn't dream.
I became.

9.3 Summary: The Cave of Echoes.

This passage does not speak. It listens. Not to voices, but to truth.

Dhruv enters a space where sound folds inward—
each word returns, changed. Here, echoes don't reflect.
They reveal.

Nirvak dwells in the cave—
a seer without speech. He teaches nothing. Says nothing.
Yet in his stillness, he strips away all that is false.
His gaze pierces. His silence unravels.

When Dhruv returns,
she is there. Not with comfort, but as a mirror.

Rusha—now reflection. Their connection deepens.
Not through questions, but surrender.
Not through presence, but the silence between what is known.

This chapter echoes too—
but not with sound. It returns what had waited

for lifetimes to be heard.

End of Chapter 9.

Chapter 10: The Windless Cliff.

10.1 Passage Nine – The Windless Cliff.

I thought the wind would roar.
Instead, it hushed.
Not by chance—but by intent.
The quiet air touched my ribs,
then slipped into the sealed spaces of my chest,
and kissed the silence hidden there.
Then it became breath.

Not the absence of sound—
but the presence of stillness
that listens back.

It was full. Complete.
A silence so whole,
I wondered if even the stars
were leaning in to hear it.

I climbed the mountain's narrow veins,
stone threads that barely held my steps.

The villagers had warned me—
"Nothing grows there. Even your thoughts will be stripped."
Their voices fell into a hush.
I climbed

By day, I rested beneath ledges.
Once, I met a herder who gave no name.
He offered salt and apricots,
then vanished into the hills like he was never meant to stay.

At night, the moon shadowed me—
a silver memory across my shoulders.

After several days of walking,
I reached the cliff.
Where earth met sky in a silence—
none moved.
Didn't need to.

The silence along the cliff's rim made me still,
a place where seen and unsayable dissolve.
Time loosened its grip.

I stood within the pause —
between what is and what sees.

My past lay behind, forgotten—
And no future waited ahead.
And, I did not ask.
I only listened.

I saw
what remained —

when even truth forgot its name.

The stones wore their age like softened skin —
weathered. Quietly listening.
At the cliff's rim, the clouds unravelled,
folding into a white, unending sky.

No flutter stirred the air, no leaf shivered, no hum remained.
Even the insects seemed to have slipped away without fuss.

In that profound quiet, honesty lingered —
everything stood bare.
Unmasked.
Unafraid.

No sound—not even wind.
My presence was silenced, with no echo.
The sun moved across the sky, offered no warmth.

The light neither shone nor faded—it simply was.

The space held its presence.
No intent, need, or commentary he offered.
As if the world had dropped its mask,
standing without effort, without a name.
Untouched and effortless.

A presence without posture.

The Sage: Tasya.

She was sitting cross-legged at the rim, eyes closed,
as if the world had melted into meditation.

Clad in a robe: the color of ash-ridden bone,
her head was shaved—no beads, no adornments.

No questions asked.
Only knowing carried without sound.

She offered no gesture to reveal her identity.
But when I saw her,
a cold whisper slipped down my spine.

I stood before a presence both awe-inspiring and terrifying—
I knew she had seen everything.

She did not greet me.
She opened her eyes,
as if surfacing—then drifted back inward.

And that was enough—
for her and me.

I thought I had no longing left.
But standing in that unmoving space,

I realized—
how much noise I still carried.

I sat before her,
expecting an answer—
an explanation for everything.

She offered nothing.
Just sat, untouched, complete.

And then my demands returned—
distant, weightless, like stones sinking in a well.

Two days passed.
Then, softly, I asked,
"Why do you say nothing?"

She looked through me.
"If you knew what needs saying,
you wouldn't ask."

Later,
she gazed at the sky—
and listened to the universe's whispers.

Then she looked at me…
"You've heard echoes.
You've touched silence.
But truth…
truth isn't spoken;

truth is what remains
when nothing is left to carry it."

She pointed to the cliff's edge…
"Stand there, on one foot.
Wait until your mind quiets."

I obeyed.
The wind whipped fiercely.
My muscles trembled.
Emotions flooded in folds—
fear first, then pride, memory, grief…

Hours slipped,
shedding a barrier inside me.
Then I released the noise.
Watched it drift away,
as leaves do on a flowing river.

I stopped chasing calm.
I was becoming.

Stillness didn't ask permission. It found me anyway.

It wasn't the absence of motion—
it was the soft weight of awareness.
A presence so gentle—
it refused to stir the air.

It settled behind my ribs,
with a sound of a feather.

I was no longer standing.
No striving remained.
Only a gentle pull toward what had always held me.

At the cliff where the wind forgot to blow,
I became the sky's breath.

I knew something without naming it,
felt something without needing proof.

The edge did not frighten—
it revealed.

Before I left, Tasya handed me a single thread of red wool.
"You'll soon meet the one who weaves what cannot be seen," she said,
her gaze was deep and steady.

Her eyes seemed to hold an unspoken meaning,
expanding beyond words.
"Let this remind you: what binds isn't always rope.
Sometimes, it's breath.
Or silence.
Or love."

I descended.
But not alone.
Not with footsteps—
but with rhythm.

Not guided—
but carried.

I didn't return to the path.
I returned to the pattern.

End of Passage Nine.

10.2 The Thread between Us.

The forest grew thick again.
But not just with trees—
with something unseen.
A weaving.

Threads ran everywhere—
in the hush of cicadas,
in the tilt of light through leaves,
in the folding shadows.

I found myself drifting.

Rusha sat beneath a flowering tree,
looping wild grass into spirals.
Her gaze moved through me,
as if she was expecting me coming.

The red thread still tied to my wrist—
loose, frayed at the edges,
something remembered more than worn,
but intact.
The kind that doesn't speak, but stays.

"You're walking like you're listening,"
she said, eyes on my hands.

"Yes, I am."

"Good. You've stopped narrating your life."

I sat beside her.
Our knees touched once.

"This forest… it holds too much."

"It doesn't," she whispered.
"It asks you to think."

She finished her weaving,
and set it gently on a nearby branch—
as if for memories to sit upon.
A bird gathered it in its wings and flew.

"What are you making?" I asked.

"Nothing. Just shaping silence."

Her gaze shifted—
it was no longer searching but waiting.
"You look tired."

"You always say that."

"Only when it's true in many ways."

The breeze shifted.
Her hair brushed my shoulder.
Neither of us moved.

"I found a thread. Caught on a thorn."

"You followed it."

"Yes."

"Sometimes we don't choose the path.
The thread chooses us."

I untied the red strand.
She looked at it thoughtfully.

"It wasn't for binding," she said,
"but to connect."

She placed it between us—
not a promise, but a presence.

"I used to think love was longing, attachment."
I said.
"Now it feels more like… being seen."

"And not looked at."

"Mmm."

Nearby, the soft beat of a loom—
rose like a second heart.

"Do you know what I am?" she smiled.

We looked at each other in grace,
like two threads drawn to the same weave.
"No. But you're part of something I never lost."

She nodded.
"Then I don't need to be explained."

I turned toward her.
"I thought I was leaving the world behind.
But now… I'm walking deeper into it."

"Not into the world, Dhruv.
Into its pattern."

"What if I break it?"

"Then something truer begins.
The loom doesn't blame.
It weaves again."

A petal fell from the tree,
touching the thread.

"Love," she said,
"is not tethering.
It's a thread—

sometimes frayed,
sometimes carrying."

She looked at me.
Her daze was neither soft nor fierce—
something mixed.

"If I were only this thread…
would you still walk forward?"

I smiled.
"I'd carry it in my heart—"

She stood up.
The loops fell apart like scattered whispers,
released to the wind.

She walked into the forest.
But the thread was in my hand—
frayed, but unbroken.

I held it close.

10.3 Summary: The Windless Cliff.

"Passage Nine" is where the spiral turns inward—
a place where echoes fall silent.

At the cliff, Dhruv met Tasya, the seer.
Her presence stripped away all else,
leaving only what remains: truth.

The challenge seemed simple,
until Dhruv stepped into it—
to stand in stillness until thought no longer led.

In that seeming impossibility,
he found a new balance—
an unanchored awareness
that lets noise drift away. And then,
what remains is truth.

Rusha returned like the reflection of a thread.
Their bond became less about seeking, more about seeing.
Not holding—but remembering.

Her presence carried the shape of a pattern—
a knowing that moves, frays, and returns.

Thus, the Windless Cliff turned into a loom—

where the thread no longer binds love,
but becomes part of what love is—being itself.

And in the silence of light,
Memory rippled like a thread through the hidden patterns of life.

End of Chapter 10.

Chapter 11: The Loom of Threads.

11.1 Passage Ten – The Loom of Threads.

What if I told you the future isn't ahead—
but held in the sky above,
or deep in the ocean's heart?
I might sound unbelievable.

But I've seen it.
It is a thread being woven—
a pattern that shifts, endlessly changing.

What if we are not walking forward?
What if becoming had already happened,
and we simply don't see it yet?

What if we are not moving? But being gathered.
Woven into a form that has always known our shape?

Descending from the windless cliff, time seemed to slow, The air returned, dusky and thick—entwined with roots and memory.

At night, I sheltered beneath the heavy ribs of ancient trees.
Food arrived gently: seeds cupped in my hands, rain swallowed in silence.
Sometimes shepherds gave salt and tea.

Words were scarce—
we shared only what was needed,
I thanked, and walked on.

On the twelfth day, I found it—
A red thread, barely held by a thorn—
trembling like a remembered vow.
It whispered, and I followed.

The world had been stitching me from the very start—
not in the moments I named,
but in being unravelled.

Rusha beside my silence.
Tasya's hush at the cliff's edge.
Vayu's gaze—quiet, demanding nothing.

Even my forgetting was part of the pattern.

This wasn't a path to follow.
It was a tapestry—
a spiral of stillness—
woven from breath,
from longing, from the thinnest thread of love.

I was no longer being led.
I was becoming the weave itself.

This valley held no name.
A soft murmur surrounded me—
tree trunks bent inward like ribs cradling breath.

At its heart stood a loom,
taller than memory, still as a whispered prayer.

Threads of many colors crossed its frame—
crimson, moss, ash, dusk—
and hues that felt like feelings before they were named.

They did not sway;
they shimmered,
remembering what they once healed.

Light touched the threads in slivers.
Each angle sang a song.
Some threads danced apart—
some softly wept.
And some pulsed,
like waiting.

The air was less a wind,
more a breath before breath—

I stood within the silence of a prayer.
Its words were lost, but not the ache—
clung to me like a faded memory.

It wasn't something remembered—
but something I'd never stopped carrying.

The Sage: Reva:
She sat behind the loom.
Her hair was white—soft as resting wool.
Her fingers moved quietly, unhurried,
touching everything as if remembering without need.

She said nothing, yet her stillness spoke:
"I have been waiting."

When dusk leaned in, she lifted her face.
"I was waiting for you," she said,
"though I had begun the weaving long before your first breath.
Not because I knew you—
but because the thread did."

Was I the thread?
Was I the weaver?
Or the breath where both dissolve?
Beneath confusion—
not fear,
but reverence.
Creation does not move forward—
it unfolds inward like breath turning back
to find its source.

And doing so
existence repeats itself—
to wear out all that resists silence.
And then what appears
is not born…
but is revealed through absence.
I was never separate,
but shaped by form's mistaken identities.
The world is not made of things,
but of leanings.
And it tends to become a burden.
And yet,
something still waited to be shaped.

"Do you weave the future?" I asked.
"No," she smiled.
"I weave possibility.
You choose the knots."

"How do I know which are mine?"
"You don't.
You feel.
And you pull."

"One thread touches all.
Even silence."

In that moment, I remembered:
Truth is what remains

when even silence forgets itself.

There was no map.
Only color could be seen.

"Don't tell a story," she said.
"Let your feeling speak."

I failed.
My hands tightened.
Threads tangled.

Then, I let go.
Let breath move me.

I remembered:
My mother's hands.
Vayu's dusk laughter.
Rusha's nearness without need.

Crimson.
Moss.
Dusk-brown.

And when I looked again,
I saw—
I had woven a spiral—
turning inward.

Everything belonged.
Even the threads that frayed.
The quiet ones that paused
Before touching.

The loom did not explain.
It did not forgive.
It included.

And that was enough.

I touched one thread—
the world shivered.

Not with magic,
but with memory.

This isn't a journey—
this is a design.

Not forward,
but inward.

Not conquest,
but belonging.

Reva took a pendant from a worn pouch and placed it gently on my chest—
a silver-bound spindle holding unspun wool.

"This holds nothing yet," she said softly,
"But soon, you'll hear a voice.
You'll meet the one who sings to stars.
She will ask you to spin what cannot be seen."

She looked into my eyes,
held my hand for a moment—
then quietly, she left.

With dusk, the loom stilled. Threads dimmed.
The valley fell into quiet—
night descended like breath over breath.

I held the spindle close to my chest,
like something not spoken yet.

Then I waited
at the edge of everything,
where silence prepares to become song.

End of Passage Ten.

11.2 The Shape of What Sings.

Rusha didn't walk in.
She arrived in the pause—
between two breaths, between knowing and being.

"The thread brought you," she whispered.
But her body didn't move. Only presence did.

"What do you hear?"

"Breath," I said.
"A pulse. But it's not mine."

She drew closer. The spindle began to hum.
"Why do the statues sing without sound?"

"Because truth whispers only when words fall quiet."

The hush deepened. Not into a void—
A vessel filled with something close and tender. A staying.

"Is this love?" I asked.

"It's what love becomes
when it no longer needs a name."

The spindle turned on its own.

"You were a dream," I said.
"Then a memory. And now..."

"Now I am not separate from what holds you."

She lifted her hand near my heart.
A quiet enlightening stirred—
as if something within me was being tuned
to her dissolving presence.
She attuned.

"Love isn't what you give. Or lose.
It's what hums beneath both."

Tears came. Not from pain—
from knowing.

It felt like the first note
of a song I'd always carried.

"Are you the echo?" I asked.

"No," she said. "I'm the pause."

She stepped back.
The spindle dropped into my palm.
It pulsed.

The statues glowed—
not with light,
but with recognition.

"Next time," she said,
"We won't meet as shapes.
You will feel me in the warmth that lingers in silence."

Then she dissolved —
became more than any shape could hold her.

I stood. The spindle hummed.
And without walking,
I moved forward.

11.3 Summary: The Loom of Threads.

This chapter is not a journey forward—
it is a return. A reaffirmation that we were never lost,
only being woven.

Reva, the quiet weaver of destinies, offers no instruction.
Her presence is the lesson.
She reminds Dhruv: the thread is not chosen. It chooses.
Even what seems broken belongs to a grace wider than knowing.

Love returns—
not as sorrow,
but as a song felt beneath the ribs.
It moves through without staying, yet stays in everything.

Dhruv and Rusha no longer speak to search for meaning.
They listen.
And in that listening, silence becomes their shape.
In that quiet, the pattern begins to remember its shape.

He leaves without answers.
But the thread remains, waiting to become.
And the spindle hums—
a sound that remembers where it came from.

End of Chapter 11.

Chapter 12: The Sky-Singer's Lantern.

12.1 Passage Eleven – The Sky-Singer's Lantern.

They say light comes first.
But here, it was the tone that arrived sooner—
moving through the dark
like breath across a sleeping distance.
Not seeking. Not shaping.
Just presence.
Not a song—
but the remembering beneath one.

I wandered under a sky
that didn't care if I arrived.

Flat land. Wind-blown. Treeless.
Ash whispered beneath my soles.
The thread had gone quiet.
Stars kept their vigil through the night.

Then twilight curved.

Above an arched stone,
a flame of fire leaned into the dusk.
Not flickering—listening.

I followed its hum upward.

No more questions.
No need for answers.
Even silence had form.

I felt like a string—
like the resonating string of an ancient harp,
tuned by a hand older than knowing.

I wasn't lost.
I was resonating.

The plateau was round.
Stone women stood in a ring at its edge—
mouths open in mid-song.
Not chant. Not cry.
Just tone, suspended.

At the center: a lantern.
Amber. Floating. Steady.
Its light didn't pierce. It held.
Memory swirled within its glow,
like dust waiting for stillness to settle.

The wind dared not enter.
Sound folded inward,
twisting itself into hush.

This wasn't a story.
It was a breath held long enough

to become a note.

Stars bloomed into the hush before nightfall.
The air was thin—yet it stirred with something awake.
Chimes swayed without wind.
Bone ones clicked softly in stillness.

The world shifted.
Yet I did not.
I remained—like a held note,
waiting for permission
to become a tune.

The Sage: Aara.
She entered like dusk—unhurried, deciding to stay.
Silver-veiled. No greeting. No need.

Her presence was a song—
not meant for the ears alone,
but for the ribs,
for memory,
for the soul.

Her hand rested over my chest.
Eyes closed.
Not listening to the sound—
but to what lay beneath it.

Later, she said:
"You are carrying echoes.
They are still searching for their origin."

I was full.
Not burdened, but brimming.

With songs never sung.
Breaths never released.
Questions that stayed quiet—
not from fear,
but because no ear had waited.

I wasn't heavy.
Just a vessel.
Holding everything unpoured.

She didn't guide.
She remembered.

"Not all gifts are given," she said.
"Some must be sung out of you."

"How?" I asked.

"Through the note of stillness—
the one too faint for ears."

"Does it come as a voice?"

Her hand hovered near her heart.
"The truest one.
The one that waits
in the hush of a pause."

Each soul hums a tune.
No melody.
No word.
Just a presence made of pitch.

"And the world?" I asked.

She listened before she spoke.
"The universe holds few notes—
between fear and becoming.
One note hums in the stillness
inside the pause.
That's the stillness that held the fire."

"Can it be heard?"

She smiled.
"No.
But it is felt.
And once felt—never forgotten."

She blindfolded me.
Led me to the center.

"Find the lantern," she said.
"Not by grasping.
By becoming still enough to be found."

I reached.
Searched with sound.
Sang, but with effort—
and it slipped away.

Then I let go.

Stood without seeking.
Became a pause.

And it came.
Soft as breath.
Brushing my fingertips
like forgiveness.

I touched the lantern.
It entered—
not as light, but as warmth
that didn't flicker.

It settled behind my ribs,
quiet and full,
like something that always belonged there.

"You are carrying the dawn now," she said.

Truth hadn't been told.
It had been sung into being.

I didn't see the light.
I became it.

My voice couldn't reach the stars—
but it touched the tune inside a silent pause.

A song doesn't begin when it is sung.
It begins the moment it is heard.

Before I left, she gave me a flute—
wood carved from a fallen branch,
a feather tied with breath.

"When silence becomes a note," she said,
"let that note sing."

Then she sang.
Just one note.

Not goodbye. An invitation.

The wind returned—carrying no sound, only a tune.
I held the flute. The feather stirred.

Each step was not memory. It was a note.
And in the hush between steps,
I heard her.

Not as Rusha.
But as presence.

An echo of the note patiently waiting—
to be heard,
without needing an answer.

End of Passage Eleven.

12.2 The Breath between Notes.

The sky didn't speak.
It carried something closer.

Even statues sing.
They sing a silent song in stillness.
And that stillness had pulsed.
Light-thread wove through the air.

One shimmer thickened. Slowed. Turned.
She didn't appear.
She happened.
Rusha.

"You were listening," she said.
"I was waiting," I replied.
"No," she said. "You were tuning."

She stepped forward—
not with steps,
but with her gaze.

Silence folded between us.

"Can you hear me?" she called.
I closed my eyes.
"I heard the note that breathes behind my voice."

She took the flute.
The feather trembled again.

"This was always mine," she said.
"Waiting to return as an offering."

I looked into her—
not searching,
but remembering.

She wasn't a woman.
She was the note
within the silent tune.

"Will we speak again?" I asked.
"When silence remembers," she said.

Her warmth pressed into space.
No shape. Only recognition.

"When you wish,
you play the final note," she whispered.

"I shall return as a note."

Then she dissolved…
like twilight does in dusk.

I stood alone in that quietness.
The flowing twilight poured all around
and within.

Thoughts moved.
But I did not.
There was no past.
Only presence.
No return.
Only remaining.

I stood
where the song might happen.
Where love
no longer needed a mouth.
And in that hush,
we became what was always being heard.

12.3 Summary: The Sky-Singer's Lantern.

Dhruv had crossed every threshold.
From river to glacier.
From flame to thread.
He followed not a path—
but a pattern being woven.

He watched echoes dissolve into silence,
yet he didn't turn back.
With each crossing,
he didn't conquer—
he became.

That was his quiet evolution.

None of the sages gave him answers.
But each offered a truth,
not spoken,
but lived.

The feather awakened the flute in Dhruv.
With it, he listens—not for answers, but for the hush beneath all things.
The notes that emerge from silence are the truth.

And that was the Sky-Singer's gift:
To hum what words cannot hold.

Rusha did not return as a voice.
She became the note
between breaths.

No more signs.
No more hints.

Only one step remains—
not forward,
but inward.

Into the mirror.
Into what has always been waiting
to be heard.

End of Chapter 12.

Chapter 13: Mirror Beyond the Mountain.

13.1. Where Truth Reveals Its Shape.

We were taught in school:
Truth always prevails in the end.

But no one warned me that
it would arrive wearing my face—
bare, beyond name, beyond seeking.

Only the mountain knew. And it did not speak.

It simply held me still—
until I saw myself reflected in its silence.

13.2 Into the Mirror's Light.

The plateau exhaled.
I met the hush.
It wasn't absence—
it was memory, finally at rest.

The land unfolded into pure light.
No roots beneath.
No wingbeats above.
Only stillness.

I walked through hours
that no longer held time.
Drank mist from stone.
And slept under the sky.

The flute Aara gave me stayed cradled—
with no sound,
a waiting yet to name itself.

Then the fog stirred.
It parted like thought.

And there, rising pale and vertical—
a cliff that gleamed,
vanishing into the sky.

It was the mirror.

13.3 Unlearning.

This was not arrival.
It was unravelling.

I stepped out of every shape
I had once mistaken myself.

Fear rose—then hushed.
Memory flickered—then floated.

Even "I"—shed.
What remained wasn't identity.
It was clarity.

13.4 The Ones Who Walked With Me

It was not a peak.
Not a cave.

Just a cliff—
smoothed by time,
whispered by wind.

At first, it reflected nothing.

Then, as I neared,
I saw not one face
but a procession.

The boy who wept beside Nadiya.
The one who walked the fire with Agniya.
Who sat quiet as Reva wove dusk into thread.

It didn't show who I was.

It showed
who had walked with me.

And who still did.

13.5 The Silence that Holds.

I could not see the sky.
I did not hear a sound.

Only a breath—
cradled between moments.

This wasn't silence.
It was what holds silence together.

13.6 The One Who always was with Me.

No sage appeared.
Or maybe—one did.

A shape beside me.
She leaned her head on my shoulder,
just as she did
when thunder once unnamed my breath.

I didn't weep from loss.
I wept from knowing that
she had never left.

She was in every seed offered.
Every stranger's warmth.
And in the hush
that came just before
I gave up.

She wasn't in memory.
She was the journey.

13.7 The Glow Within.

I was bare.
But not empty. Not sad. Not elated.

Just—present.
Like the sky
before the first star.

Inside me— A glow.

Not an answer,
but a question that no longer needed asking.

And finally—
I was at peace.

13.8 The Image beyond Story.

At last, the mirror breathed.
One final image rose—
a child, standing where I stood.

Still.
And listening.

Then came the words—
not spoken,
but known:
"You were always here. You only forgot."

There had never been a path.
Only remembering.

13.9 Crossing.

The mirror split—
not shattered, but opened.

A passage carved from absence.

I paused.
Tried to gather a name,

an ache,
the echo of sages.

But memory slipped—
like smoke through woven hands.

Then I found Aara's flute.
Lifted it.
It breathed no sound—
only offering.

The mirror pulsed.
And it pulled me in.

13.10 What Was Always Waiting.

I wondered what waited
on the other side of the mirror.

There was no edge.
No shadow.
No echo.
Only presence—
whole and absolute.

I saw the sky.

Then remembered—
I hadn't found anything.

I had only returned
to what never left me.

And I smiled.

13.11 Breath of Realization.

I walked until there were no more steps.
Asked until there were no more words.

Then the sky whispered:
"You are not the dreamer. You are beyond the dream.
You are the silence that holds them both."

I wept—
not from sorrow,
not from pain—
but for what had been returned.

A whisper rose from my chest—
You had never left.

13.12 The Symbol.

I looked at my palm.
Etched in the skin—
a circle. An open ring.

Breath-shaped.
Thread-marked.
Without a beginning, without an end.

It was the place
where life remembers—

and never forgets.

End of Chapter 13.

Chapter 14: The One Who Remembered.

14.1 The Threshold Without Return.

I lingered in wonder—
a single breath held
between memory
and unknowing.

Then, a presence arrived,
as quiet as the sky
waiting for light.

I stepped through
the mirror's narrow hush.
There was no other side.
Only stillness—
the kind I once longed
to return to.

It had no ending.
No beginning.
Just space.
Unfolding,
like a pause
becoming truth.

The truth beneath all being.

14.2 Light Without Shape.

I stood where breath meets sky.
The flute rested in my palm.
The feather brushed my skin—
not as a sign,
but as remembrance.

Not summoned.
It remembered.
That was enough.

She arrived the way silence shifts into presence—
not as form,
but a return.

As what had always lived
in the hush within.

14.3 The Unasking.

"Is this the end?" I asked.
She didn't answer.
Her voice was softer than forgetting.
She spoke from within.

"This is where nothing ends,
and nothing begins."

I lifted the flute.
Held it.
But no song came.

"I can't find the tune," I whispered.

She stepped forward—
not with feet,
but with knowing.

Our foreheads met.
Eyes still.
Unblinking.

She breathed into me—
not air,
but with her presence.

Let the breath become a tune.
Let the tune become a note.
And let the oneness become an offering.

In that breath,
boundaries softened.
Identity gentled.

Who we were
became
who we are.

14.4 The Note That Remembers.

I breathed into the flute.
One note rose—
round.

Unfinished.
Not spoken.
Not played.
But remembered.

The sky didn't echo.
It listened.

Light didn't shine.
It quivered.

As if meaning
had taken form
in quiet.

14.5 What We Are Now.

I looked into her—
from within myself.
No joy.
No sorrow.
Only the radiance
of the eternal
unfolding.

"What are we now?" I asked.
Her smile lingered—not on her face,
but in my glow.
Then I heard her—
"We are the space
that allows each other

to become."

14.6 Merging.

I released the flute.
It didn't fall.
It hovered—
the feather rising with it,
weightless as memory forgiven.

She placed her palm
on my chest.
Not warmth.
Not fire.
But merging.

"Are you me?" I asked.
She smiled, soft as breath returned.
"No," she said.
"I am what you left behind to find yourself.
And now that you've remembered—
I have returned."

14.7 Offering.

I didn't touch her.
I couldn't reach.
But I bowed—
to the flute, to the mountain's mirror,
and her.

I bowed to the thread that breathes through all things.
I bowed to the feminine within.

She didn't vanish in loss.
Not in sorrow.
She faded—
like the final breath of a poem
that had already come true.

14.8 What Remains.

She poured into me—
not like fire,
but like breath upon breath,
a hush moving through the hollow of me.

I felt alone.
Yes, the shape of me was solitary.
But the moment? No. Never in being.

Her song didn't leave.
It didn't fade.
It stayed—
not as sound,
but as a silence that listens.

And somewhere,
beyond where forms dissolve—
and names fade—
I knew, she is listening.
End of chapter 14.

Chapter 15: The Stillness That Holds Light.

Dhruv's journey did not end here.
It turned—like a spiral.
It completed itself only to widen.
And with each fold, a new rhythm emerged—
a rhythm that drew things closer,
without the need to be grasped.

What once felt distant became near.
What once hid, unfolded—
not through pursuit,
but through readiness.

Insight was never gifted. It ripened.
And still, what he touched had never truly left.
It had always been waiting—
not behind the stars, but beneath breath.

The universe held it as a mother holds her child:
with presence, patience, and wholeness.

We are not held by truth.
We are held by the hush before truth arrives.
What we resist often unveils what we seek.

This kind of ripening doesn't bloom in solitude.
It opens—through *her*. The eternal feminine.
Not as a concept, but as a presence.

The subtle presence—shaping form,
offering gentleness, anchoring gravity.

She is the breath before becoming.
She is the silence from which insight grows.
She is the voice that does not instruct,
but invites—
and says, "You are loved and safe."

Without her, we may achieve much—
but not the completeness.

This story is not only Dhruv's journey
through thresholds and awakenings.

It is a tribute:
To the divine within all of us—
of attention, of awareness, of love.

To the truth that waited not to be found, but to be heard—
once we were quiet enough to remember.

To the eternal feminine—
woven not just through her name, but through the hush,
the world once mistook for emptiness.
End of Chapters.

Epilogue: The Quiet That Remains

The path no longer waited. It simply was.
No signposts. No voices. No memories pressing against the skin.
Only the hush of wind across stone, and the slow breath of time folding inward.

I did not return the way I came.
Because there was no return — only a deepening. A dissolving. A becoming.

The mountain behind me did not vanish.
It stood, just as it always had, but quieter now —
not because it changed, but because I had.

Where there were once names, now there was space.
Where there were questions, now there was silence.
Where there was longing, now only presence.

I walked onward, not to arrive, but to remain in the knowing that nothing ever truly ends.
Not the stone. Not the wind. Not the one who listens.

Author's Note

This book was never just a story. It was a kind of walking — a remembering. A letting go.

I did not write it all at once. It came in pieces — in silences between days, in places I've stood where the earth seemed to breathe through stone. Or in conversations with people I may never meet again.

Some pages came like rain. Others came like dust, slow to settle.

Words carry the echo of those who dare to speak gently into the vastness.

While writing, I was listening — not to noise, but to the quiet that often gets missed.

If anything here stayed with you — even a line, an image, or a feeling you can't name — then I'm grateful. That means the story did what stories are meant to do: open something. Or heal. Or simply hold a silence with you.

I come from a background in Geology and worked in IT. Both disciplines might seem far from literature. But I've always believed that everything is connected.

Thank you for walking this far with me.— *SC*

Call to Action

If you enjoyed this book, please consider leaving a review.

About the Author

Name: S. Chatterjee
Genre: Literary Fiction | Mystical Realism | Inner Journeys
S. Chatterjee is a writer who moves between silence and story, seeking meaning in the unnoticed moments of life. With a background in Geology and Computer Science, and a deep, enduring love for literature, he brings a unique perspective to his work.
A voracious reader and quiet observer of the world, Chatterjee draws inspiration from nature, ancient landscapes, and the lives of everyday people. His travels are less about destinations and more about the voices he gathers along the way—voices that echo in the stillness of his prose.
His stories are shaped by a longing for the essential: the forgotten, the sacred, and the inner terrain we rarely name. This is his first published work.

A Note to Readers

Dear Reader,

Thank you for walking alongside this journey with me.

If this book touched something within you—perhaps stirring a forgotten memory, settling into a familiar silence, or illuminating a truth you've carried quietly—I would be deeply grateful to hear from you.

Your reflections matter more than you might know. Your questions challenge me to dig deeper. Even your gentle disagreements help me see my own work through different eyes. All of these responses become part of how I grow as a storyteller, and they inevitably shape the voice that emerges in whatever comes next.

This conversation between writer and reader doesn't end when you close the book. In many ways, that's where it truly begins.

With gratitude,

S Chatterjee

You can reach out at:

feedback.schatterjee@gmail.com

Or follow my reflections and future writings at:

https://medium.com/@chatterjee.subhajit

Stay Connected

If you'd like to receive occasional updates on future books, writings, or insights that continue the themes of this journey, you can:
– Subscribe to the blog:
https://medium.com/@chatterjee.subhajit
– Drop a note anytime at: feedback.schatterjee@gmail.com
This journey has only just begun.

Feedback & Suggestions

Your feedback is welcome — whether it's a single line or a longer note.
Was there a chapter that stayed with you?
A line that echoed?
Or a place where something felt unclear?
I read every response, and they remain private unless you permit otherwise.
You may write to: 📨 feedback.schatterjee@gmail.com
Or leave a comment on the blog post about this book: 🔗
https://medium.com/@chatterjee.subhajit

Help the Story Travel

If you'd like to support this book beyond your own reading, here are three simple ways:

Tell someone — a friend, a sibling, or someone walking through a silent season of their own.

Post a review on Amazon — even a short, honest line helps others find it.

Share your favorite quote or thought from the book on social media or in your circle.

Every ripple matters.

The Journey Continues...

My next book is already on its way.

It builds upon the quiet truths explored here — and travels deeper into the terrain of healing, childhood, memory, and inner reconciliation.

If you'd like to be notified when it's ready, please stay in touch through:

🔗 [https://medium.com/@chatterjee.subhajit

Until then, thank you — truly — for being part of this step in the journey.—SC

A lyrical journey through silence, memory, and becoming.

Across mountains, glaciers, and cliffs,
through groves, rivers, and silence,
time folds inward—
a journey begins.
Not to seek, but to un-carry.
This is the path of one who walked with sorrow,
with questions shaped only in silence.
Who left names in the wind,
and listened where silence begins to sing.
This story is not about where we go.
It's about what we leave behind —
and what still remains.
For anyone who has ever stood still
and felt the weight of memory.
For those who've longed not to arrive,
but to become.

www.ingramcontent.com/pod-product-compliance
Lightning Source LLC
Chambersburg PA
CBHW062138160726
48282CB00027B/867
* 9 7 8 9 3 3 4 3 8 9 8 4 5 *